Learning to Sit in the

S I L E N C E

A Journal of Caretaking

Also by Elaine Marcus Starkman

The Best Time
Love Scene

Learning to Sit in the

S I L E N C E

A Journal of Caretaking

ELAINE MARCUS STARKMAN

Papier-Mache Press
Watsonville CA

ISBN: 0-918949-43-2 Softcover
ISBN: 0-918949-44-0 Hardcover

Cover art, "Fullness," fabric and thread, © 1992 by Deidre Scherer from the collection of Susan and Lawrence Bailis
Cover design by Cynthia Heier
Photo by Leon Starkman
Typography by Prism Photographics

Grateful acknowledgment is made to the following publications which first published some of the material in this book:

Across the Generations (California Arts Council, 1982); *Ariadne's Thread: A Collection of Contemporary Women's Journals* (Harper Row, 1982); *Women and Aging: An Anthology by Women* (Calyx, 1986); *Filtered Images: Women Remembering Their Grandmothers* (Vintage '45 Press); *Kalliope: A Journal of Women's Art*, Vol. 9, No. 3; *Love Scene* (SheerPress); *Moment*, Vol. 8, No. 2, 1983; and *Womanblood* (Continuing Saga Press, 1981).

Library of Congress Cataloging-in-Publication Data

Starkman, Elaine Marcus
    Learning to sit in the silence : a journal of caretaking / Elaine Marcus Starkman.
        p.   cm.
    ISBN 0-918949-44-0 : $14.00 — ISBN 0-918949-43-2 (soft) : $9.00
    1. Aging parents—Care—United States. 2. Caregivers-United States—Psychology. 3. Women—United States—Diaries. 4. Adult children—United States—Family relationships. I. Title.
HQ1063.6.S73   1993
306.874—dc20   93-28204
                                                                          CIP

Acknowledgments

With appreciation to Susan Aglietti of Vintage '45 Press for her belief in these pages; with thanks to Sandra Hershkowitz and Sunny Solomon, two superb and trusted proofreaders; to Leon for his encouragement and sense of fairness when I've felt myself too self-indulgent; to my grown children, their spouses, and their friends who, hopefully, will look back at this period of our lives with understanding and good humor; and to Sara Wallach and all those unnamed friends and relatives who cared.

In memory of my father, David Samuel Marcus, 1905-1991
And my mother-in-law, Blanche Milstein Starkman, 1900-1991

And for my grandsons—
Andrew, born in 1990, and David, born in 1992

Learning to Sit in the

SILENCE

A Journal of Caretaking

Introduction

When my mother-in-law had been living with us about a week, I decided to keep a journal of everything she said or did. I saw her as a link in a chain of generations, one of the last from the "old country" in our family. With no great purpose in mind, I simply wanted to capture and preserve her mode of thought and the colorful way she spoke. Until the age of eighty, she'd managed on her own as a landlady in an urban neighborhood, but after a fire gutted her apartment, she became disoriented and intermittently stayed with her two children who resided in the same area. Eventually, she came to settle with us. As the weeks passed, I began recording my reactions—and those of my family—to her.

A journal writer myself, I'd always been a reader of women's diaries. One of my favorites is *Revelations: Diaries of Women*, edited by Mary Jane Moffat and Charlotte Painter. I delighted in Sophia Tolstoy's exasperating comments on living with her brilliant, eccentric husband and Emily Carr's honest musings on aging. What courage these women had!

Although I'd kept journals for about twenty-five years, I'd often censored them. Later when I read them, they mirrored back emotions I was unaware of at the time of writing. Sometimes I'd start stories and finish poems from a line that had caught my eye. But not until I became engrossed in the "mother-in-law diaries" was I able to capture those emotions I felt in a fleeting moment—and to express love, jealousy, anger, and guilt more fully.

Three years ago I spent seven weeks at Ragdale Foundation in Lake Forest, Illinois. There I began editing the hundreds of pages that I'd accumulated over the years. I collapsed time and weeded out Ma's various moves back and forth across the country, as well as deleted long, self-indulgent passages, which I'd originally needed to free my work.

Other thoughts had begun to spill into "Ma's diary"; the entries took on a life of their own. This time I didn't hold back but moved in the direction they pulled me—my awareness of how the elderly are treated became heightened. Through journal-keeping I began to learn about the politics of aging; I began to face the absence of ground rules, trying to create ones that were livable for me. My journal not only became a history of my response to Ma's decline, but also a statement on my own aging.

While this book is autobiographical in many ways, the dates, places, names, and circumstances have all been fictionalized to protect the privacy of those concerned. And while most of the entries occurred, I have taken writer's license to concentrate only on those situations which directly involved my own family after Ma settled with us and to shape them as I wish. Last, I have edited some of my mental ramblings to make them more accessible to readers.

A journal can distort a picture of a person's life; no writer is the sum total of any one journal—she is also what remains unexpressed. Claire Brenner is one persona of myself, one who is younger, more naive, and less able to separate herself from others than her present creator. Narrator and author resemble one another, but they are not identical. Two years have passed since Ma's death; I remember her with great fondness and respect, as do my four children, now grown, and, needless to say, my husband who often played the greater nurturer than I. I remember her wit and wisdom, her ability to give unconditional love and to accept life's adversities.

There are changes in our family I thought would never happen: the loss of one of my own parents; the decline of the other; the freedom of a quiet house allowing me to write whenever I want; a few wrinkles; two grand-children of my own; and, hopefully, more understanding about the life process of aging.

After all these years, I have a room of my own and a new method of journaling. With my left-handed scribbling I could never write in those beautiful hardbacks one buys in good stationery stores, but I no longer have dozens of faded spiral notebooks lying around either. I've begun to keep my journal on the computer. Late at night I fumble into my room, turn off the lights, flip the switch, close my eyes, pound away, and wait for surprises.

Once, ten years ago, I wrote: "Why are my actions so different from my thoughts?" With the publication of *Learning to Sit in the Silence,* the gap has begun to close.

Elaine Marcus Starkman
June 1993

1987

I got everything I need

April 27, 1987

Since her arrival last night, Ma's been sleeping on and off all day. The time difference, the climate change, the new environment, have exhausted her. Either that, or she's escaping through sleep.

It's difficult to know how much she's capable of, but we do know she can't manage alone any longer. Maury's sold the small apartment building she and Pa owned since the fifties. She's spent the last six months shuffling between his brother and sister; now she's here. Didn't have the heart to ask how long she will stay.

These past two days I've been thinking a lot about aging. Will I take on a new personality as I age—or intensify the one I already have?

Some elderly men and women become irritable, but Ma's become fearful of asking for anything and a lot quieter than she was in her landlady years. She doesn't complain or demand. Her response is as always, "Everything works out." She's a woman without gall.

April 28

Not sure how old Ma is, maybe eighty-two. During her seventies she was fine, now this slow disintegration. Why do some people age more slowly than others? Is it something they do to themselves? Heredity? A life-style they cultivate?

I'm unsettled by her traditional female responses, how she's always lived her life for others. And now she seems like an empty shell. She *does* have herself, she *does* have the love and respect of her three children, even though two of them can't manage her care.

How hard the move has been for her. Hope there's not too much upset with the rearrangement of the kids' bedrooms.

April 30

Since Amy's the youngest, looks like she gets the pull-out couch in the dining room until Karen goes away to college. Then she can take Karen's space and move in with Lori. Jon gets to keep his own room. He needs somewhere to study for his classes at college this semester while he works part-time.

Amy's sleeping on the couch for a few months isn't so terrible. Slept on one myself growing up, but it's less common in middle-class families nowadays.

So far the kids have adjusted to Ma better than I have, but they're gone most of the day. They aren't responsible for her the way I am. I'm too anxious about her.

May 3

Gave Ma her first bath today. I've never bathed an older person before. Although her face is very wrinkled, and for a small woman she's heavier than I thought, her body is not unattractive, though she's the last to know it. I comment, "You must have been beautiful when you were young."

"The boys liked me more than my sisters, but not because of beauty."

"Then why?"

"I had more sense; I had more patience. But now look at me."

I was touched by how difficult the simple task of bathing is for her.

May 14

A headache this morning. Seeing Ma do nothing is my hang-up, *not* hers. I try to find tasks to occupy her, give her some old sewing, spend some unwilling time with her in the kitchen. Maury brings her books to read. She prefers Yiddish books to English, reads about an hour a day. Mostly she does nothing, which makes me edgy. I have to readjust my thinking; for her, time isn't as urgent as it is for me.

Her presence stirs my memories—my two grandfathers float about, one smoking from his plastic yellow filter, staring into space, the other falling into a depression when he had to live with my uncle and give up his independence.

Ma must know the truth of May Sarton's words in *Recovering: A Journal*: "There comes a time when one must rescind authority, allow others to care for you." A terrible blow, and here Ma arrives just at the time when I'm reevaluating concepts of success and failure and what constitutes a good life—for myself.

May 15

A lovely Sunday spring day. Ma's in a sundress, sitting on the chaise lounge in the yard. She enjoys the butterflies and hints of gold creeping into the green hills. Her small dark eyes are closed, her perfect small nose blistering, her thin white hair blows around her head like a silver halo. How she loves sun. Smiley, warned not to jump on her, approaches cautiously, buries his nose in her lap and sniffs. At first she was afraid of him; she still associates dogs with pogroms and cossacks. But Smiley is more gentle than usual, and she allows him to befriend her.

When he peed on a bush she laughed, "Better than a toilet; it goes right into the dry earth." Then she stroked him and told him in Yiddish, "I too had a pet when I was young. A goat named Teibele, a sweet thing."

Maury brought out a recorder and taped her stories. She droned into it for a long time with pleasure. He has a strong bond with her; I doubt his siblings share it. When he's home, he has a need to be her caretaker.

May 18

Three weeks and the novelty has worn off. Amy complains about sleeping arrangements. We had a family meeting to see if she can squeeze in with Lori and Karen. The answer: No.

May 20

Strange…At a lecture, I meet a young woman who works in a hospice. She tells me she loves her job, that the only time she feels any honest emotion is at work helping people die.

"At last there are no pretenses; I experience a reward knowing I ease them into death while all their relatives try to keep them alive."

I describe Ma's situation. "Keep her with you as long as you can." Then she disappears into the crowd.

May 24

All of the kids are on the floor around Grandma's feet playing with Amy's old Legos. From her chair, Grandma helps too. She names each piece after a long-forgotten relative and tells a story about her brother Mendel, the tailor, Itchka, the dunce in her village, Vera, the town beauty. The kids listen as if she were spinning a fairy tale.

May 25, Memorial Day Weekend

> *She's C / not Mrs. B / that title died ten years ago / at a beach in Santa Cruz / at the shore she welled up with hatred / tore off that tag she loved / and flung it in the sand / he pulled his hair / their kiddies cried / tears stung her eyes / all of them survived / and drove home—together / now when they go to Santa Cruz / they take along Grandma*

May 29

For a treat, I took Ma to have her hair done today. On the way, she tripped and fell over the curb. She made a joke out of it and laughed, but I felt awful because I hadn't slowed my pace adequately.

"Don't worry, Claire darling. I fell at Arnold's all the time. I even tripped down some stairs."

I don't tell her that's why she's come to live with us.

I left her while her hair was drying and went home for an hour. For the first time in a month, the house felt empty without her. It's not so bad, three generations living together. We're heading for those times again with inflation, longevity, and all the changes in health care.

June 4

My friends are wrong. They don't know the benefits of having an older person around. Ma is the transmitter of our heritage and culture. The kids are learning a lot from her. Right now they're far more interested in what she has to say than in what I do! Last night she told them more stories of her brothers and sisters—Anna, Pincus, Shoshie, Mendel—the village in Poland where she'd lived as a girl, her early days in America, first as a dressmaker and a storekeeper, then as a landlady.

Most of the time, the kids are good for her; she enjoys their boisterous antics, but we're far from "The Brady Bunch." I've begun to sense some hostility. Mostly they feel their space is impinged on.

"Whose idea was this anyway?" Lori asks. "Yours or Dad's?"

"Dad's."

"How come you didn't have anything to say?"

"Dad asked me, and I agreed. Besides, she's not living with us forever; she's just staying here for a while."

"How long's she gonna stay?"

I don't answer. Maury says she "failed" at both Helen's and Arnold's; neither of them is willing to keep her any longer, but how long will *I* want to keep her?

June 8

At dinner tonight, Ma pushed her fish away. "This stinks. Did the fish man pass off a bad one onto you?"

I couldn't help laughing. "I don't have a 'fish man.' I bought it in the supermarket. Maybe you don't like the way it's spiced."

"The spices are good; the fish is bad."

She dumped her whole dinner onto Maury's plate, an annoying habit; it's not the first time. "Thank you for supper, I don't like it."

"Would you like something else?" I asked half apologetic, half annoyed.

"No, darling. I am not a pig. My stomach is small." She nibbled some bread, then got up and walked away from the table.

"How come Grandma picked the fish with her fingers when you told me not to?" asked Amy.

"She forgot she had a fork."

A few minutes later Ma returned. "Every day people saw me, knew me by my name. 'Hello, Mrs. Hilda Brenner, the nice landlady.' 'Good morning Mrs. Brenner, you give us plenty of heat. You're not like the other cheaters.' Who takes care of the building now?"

Maury explained once again. While she was with Arnold, she was vehemently against the sale. "We had to give it up, Ma; you just couldn't manage it alone anymore."

The old hurt that we try to protect her from clouded her eyes. "If Arnold and Helen and you made my mind up, okay. I trust you. You're all good children; you do what's right."

Sometimes I wish she'd question more, like she used to; she's become *too* accepting. Where's the "suspicious old woman" I've read about in books?

June 10

Took Ma on my errands with me: shopping, the post office, the library. She dragged behind so slowly, I don't have the patience to try it again....Well, maybe one more time.

June 13

Karen's high school graduation. Ma dresses. Though I don't like her mismatched outfit—a skirt from one suit and a jacket from another, the way she's knotted her stockings at the knee—I say nothing. At the Concord Pavilion a policeman brings us a wheelchair for her, and we push her up the hill. She beams when Karen walks onto the platform with six hundred other kids. "*Oy*, she's the prettiest one. That girl will go far, I'm telling you."

Karen, is it true? Is it true that you will leave all of us in the fall to start on your own path? Grandma comes, and you leave soon. Now I'll have two kids in college.

June 14

Since Ma's arrival, the TV's been on constantly.

"Shut off that damn thing!" I yell at the kids.

"Grandma likes it; she has nothing else to do."

"You could bake some cookies with her."

"She says she forgot how to bake."

"Grandma? I don't believe it."

"She likes watching TV. If you want her to bake, then you do it yourself."

"Don't give me that. Your grandmother's not going to sit in front of the boob tube all day. Not in my house."

"But she likes this program."

I walk into the family room to check out what they're viewing.

"Come watch, Claire darling. A famous woman is talking. But what has she? Not a good husband, like Maury, not a nice house like you, not beautiful children, like my grandchildren sitting here."

June 15

I must remain detached if I'm to handle Ma, accept the fact that there are no rewards, no recognition for taking care of her. I must try to go back to teaching in the fall. Can't keep taking classes and substituting on an irregular basis forever. Need to keep my mind busy. Being with her all day is not healthy for me.

June 16

We took Ma to the Jewish Home for the Aged to see about day care once a week. She detested the place, cried aloud, "I'm not like the others. I see good, I hear good, I don't make trouble for you." She thought we were leaving her there and began to cry in the director's office.

I disliked the interview with the director, a young woman with a Ph.D. and a Phi Beta Kappa plaque hanging on the wall. Distant, too professional. In a condescending tone, she asked Ma her last name, where she lived, what year it was.

On the way out, I realized that I've not been strong enough in my own stance for a professional life, whether it's insisting the kids help out or agreeing with Maury about his mother living here.

June 19

This morning Ma woke in a good mood, chewing gum and humming a beautiful Yiddish melody. I could hardly believe it. Decided she needed something to do, so I found her some potatoes; she's happily peeling them for *kugel*. Yes, here's Claire Hirsch Brenner, forty-six, who's always tried to escape the kitchen, back in it.

As we worked together in the kitchen, the remoteness of Ma's early life in Poland came alive and pervaded the air. At first I was transported, could even feel the sense of the Holocaust. For those moments it was no longer a page of history, but a reality that can't be blotted out, despite the fact that it has become an abstraction that "revisionists" claim never existed. And though I used to believe it could never happen again, there in the kitchen I felt it could.

June 20

Maury is devising ways to make life easier for Ma. We've put a chair in the bathtub; the kids grumble about removing it after she bathes. We try to involve them by asking Karen or Jon to write the date on the blackboard in her room. To our surprise, Lori's the one who's been doing it without our knowing.

June 23, 11:00 P.M.

> *Their careful English fell to common Yiddish curses / spouted from*
> *back fences of old-country memory / in the new apartment: /*
> *"Crazy one! Ride your broom back to Poland!" / "Grow like an*
> *onion your head in the ground!" / Then he smacked the little*
> *jewels / as they hid behind her skirt. / He stormed onto the porch, /*
> *a refuge from her and the past. / She flew into the kitchen, / wiped*
> *her eyes on the red kerchief: / Let him curse with fat man's tongue*
> *and small mind / but the jewels, don't touch / or she who'd never*
> *crush a bug would kill him with her soup! / Then, kerchief tucked*
> *in / she called the brood to dinner, bowled out hot borscht and*
> *ordered, / "Eat!" / Shame burning in his eyes and on his tongue /*
> *he ate while the jewels / smiled slyly into their soup.*

June 25

Didn't feel like bathing her tonight. I don't want to take away all responsibility from her, but was afraid she'd fall. Maury got Amy to help. Amazed to see a thirteen-year-old bathe her grandmother. Her naturalness with Grandma is far superior to my adult "concern." *Blessed be the child,* even if she complains about sleeping in the dining room.

June 30

Last Thursday I began driving Ma to the Senior Citizens Club at the Jewish Community Center (JCC). Maury's applied for a handicapped placard so I can park close to the entrance and she won't have to walk so far. She doesn't want to go anywhere; even at the JCC she hangs back, unwilling to socialize, says, "My business is nobody's business."

She once handled large sums of money as a businesswoman; it was humbling to watch her count in Yiddish the few pennies for lunch at the Center. Maury says it's good for her to think she's still in control, to let her pay so she won't walk around intoning, "What a poor mensch am I. Not a penny in my purse."

July 2

Maury leaves and comes home early on Tuesdays so he can take Ma to the JCC in the city and bring her back by 2:00 P.M. At first she refused to go, but now she's getting used to it. Anxiously, she waits in her chair for him. She's so proud when she returns with secondhand *shmattes* she buys for the kids—awful old spotted sweaters and dated skirts they won't wear. I end up giving them away. "Let her do it," Maury insists. "It's therapy for her."

In the past, I've never paid attention to such programs, but now I see how vitally important they are, how they must become a larger part of the national budget, available to seniors everywhere.

July 9

Today when Ma came home from the JCC, she was animated, her face red, alert. She suddenly began speaking of her childhood. "All my sisters, they didn't want to learn, but not me. I wanted to. I loved school. I had Polish school, a private Hebrew teacher, and Mendel used to bring me books by Sholom Aleichem. I read them aloud to the others. Learning's important, yes, Claire darling? You like books too."

Her tone sounded as if she was trying to please me.

Her memories of Pa were kinder than during his long illness when she was burdened by the work he couldn't do. I asked her if she'd ever considered remarrying.

"For what? To sleep with some old cocker and wash his clothes so he can take my money?"

Karen overheard and burst into laughter.

July 10

The kids have been out of school for three weeks; the noise level is driving me bats. We've no summer plans. Don't Helen and Arnold ever think *I* might like a break?

July 11

Maury spends more time with her than he does with me. Does his devotion stem from the fact that she nurtured him with unconditional love? Hate to admit it, but am disappointed in myself; I feel both jealous and guilty.

July 12, Maury's Birthday

> *I can't give you this card / you won't think it's funny / I'll get angry and you'll get angrier / even buying you a card / is like all the work / we make of love*

July 13, Midnight

Voices from the kitchen. Lori, Karen, and Ma.

Maury and I lie silently in bed, listen, don't say a word. We decide not to get up.

"Can I help you, Grandma? What are you looking for?"

"Open the kitchen door, Lori darling. I want to go out into the garden."

"Now? It's late."

"Late doesn't matter when you're old."

"But it's time to sleep."

"In my grave I'll have plenty of sleep. Now I want to see those pretty pink flowers that smell so good."

"Those are camellias, Gram, and they don't smell. And those few flowers outside aren't really a garden."

"For me they smell. For me they are a garden."

In a few minutes, we hear the shuffling of house shoes in the hall; our daughters put Grandma back to bed, quietly close their door, and talk in hushed voices for a long time.

July 14

Took Ma to the Center today where there was a lecture on the three classifications of the elderly: the "young" elderly, the "middle-aged" elderly, and the "frail" elderly. I'd never thought about these distinctions, but from the way part of the group was telling ribald jokes and planning for a trip to Reno, I could see there was certainly nothing frail about them. The director must have divided the people into their respective groups, because Ma was in a different room when I came for her. Did me good to see how vital some of them are and how much they enjoyed themselves. People really do remain young for a long time nowadays.

July 18

Wanted to run from the sound of Ma's slippers scuffing along the floor this morning—a constant reminder of age and weakness and all I must yet accomplish in my own life. Friends say it's not how *I'm* adjusting to Ma's presence, but how Maury is. Today he took her to the JCC for Sunday brunch. He asked me to come along; I was stubborn and refused.

Part of me says these trips don't matter; another part feels it's vitally important to get her to socialize, despite her own reluctance.

July 30

Ma taught me a sentence today. Sounds something like this: *Cholodno, golodno, edadamu, deloko.* "I'm tired and hungry and far from home." Think it's a dialect of Russian. She pulled it out of thin air while she was sitting in the living room. When she stares into space, her mind isn't empty after all, but filled with rich remembrances.

August 1

Along with Ma, I now drive three seniors to the JCC. A fourth from Diablo Heights Manor begs me to take her too, but the other three insist I'm "not responsible" for Mrs. G., that "she's mixed up in her brain, begs every stranger to take her out," and don't I know that the director didn't give her permission? Glad to be part of the group, Ma wags her head but refuses to lower herself to the level of gossip.

"Me, I can still remember things, thank God," she says quietly to me in private.

What *is* the place of the elderly: to beg for rides to town, to live with one's son, afraid of asking for anything? And what's my place: to oversee the situation and learn to maintain the right balance?

August 2

Hot. Grandma sits in the yard and laughs at the children's antics. "Little Jon with your big jokes, just like your grandpa, may he rest," to my nineteen-year-old. She pets our old dog who she was afraid of at first. As if he senses her fragility, Smiley refrains from jumping on her. She keeps asking for Amy, who returns from summer camp in a few days.

August 13

Bernice invited us for a swim and a light supper. When she said "bring the family," I didn't know if she meant Ma or not. Decided to drag her along. Amy balked, "Grandma eats with her fingers." Later in the car she snuggled up to Grandma, and in reversed roles, affectionately called her *"shaine punim."*

Ma had a grand time; her face beamed as she watched Amy jump off the diving board.

"A private pool in one person's yard? A heaven," she sighed.

Does she feel remorse over her life, all the years when every penny counted? Now that she has some money, she's incapable of enjoying it.

Ross spoke to her about his stamp collection as if she were a peer. So few people do. Either they're afraid of her or find her repugnant. She responded beautifully and remained alert all night, even ate two hot dogs!

When we came home, Maury wanted her to put on her nightgown right away.

"For what? I'm not tired." She stayed up until 10:30 P.M.!

August 19

Drove home the twenty miles from Berkeley like a mad woman. Imagined Ma lying dead on the floor. For the first time I escaped for a few hours only to learn there is no escape.

Came back to a mess, breakfast dishes strewn about, clothes everywhere, the stereo blasting. Karen and Ma were in the kitchen baking cookies, for which I was grateful. (It's not fair to insist the kids "baby-sit.") Jon was in his room with his girlfriend, Linda. The door was closed. A copy of *Penthouse* lay open on Ma's chair.

As I stormed in, Karen gave me one of her warnings. "Don't start raving. Grandma likes to put the flour right on the table instead of in a bowl. That way she sees just how much she's using."

"It's all over the floor. Why didn't you give her a measuring cup?"

"She wouldn't take it."

"You could have asked her to help you clean up."

"I did, but she said she's afraid to touch anything because Uncle Arnold's wife threw her out when she burnt a pot."

"Grandma never told me about that."

As I stood there gritting my teeth, Ma gave me a weak smile through flaming red lips from the lipstick the girls put on her.

"Everything's fine, darling, don't worry, everyone is good to me."

"Yeah, I dressed Grandma up. She likes that lipstick," Amy piped up.

First the kids, now the parents.

August 21

For the first time, I've used Ma's presence as a weapon to defend myself against Lori's temper.

"See, even Grandma must think you're rude."

"What does she know about your not letting me drive the car? When she first came, you said it wasn't for good."

Do the kids sense my impatience and imitate it? How can she leave? I doubt if Helen and Arnold are willing to share her care.

August 22

Apparently Karen heard Maury and Helen talking on the phone when I was out. He mentioned something to her about taking Ma next spring. I wish I knew exactly what they said. Hope she doesn't change her mind.

11:00 P.M.

Wrote both Helen and Arnold long, carefully worded letters about their obligation in sharing Ma's care. The second time I've written; I threw away the first set of letters. These I'll mail in the morning. Maury says if they don't offer, letters won't help. If I don't get any response, I'll write again next month.

August 23

I finally bought tickets for the Oregon Shakespeare Festival. After weeks of discussion, we're taking Ma along. Maury begged me. "She's never been anywhere, never seen anything since she arrived in this country."

If she doesn't come, we'll have no vacation at all. Plus we'll have to hire someone to stay here, which is expensive. Anyway, I can't bear doing that. It would hurt her. No matter how angry I get, I can't hurt her.

August 24

Home today, no mad dashing about. Ma walks into my bedroom, the one room in the house she won't enter. I pretend not to see her.

"Today my memory is a problem." She scratches her head, walks out.

Although I praise Maury to friends, tell them how much he helps with her, how she doesn't interfere with our relationship, I've felt distant from him. Right now I can't stand too much closeness.

August 25

Oh to stay in bed until noon, to escape to the ocean, to walk along the sand—to be free of her and the endless guilt. She's afraid of me, I sense it. She's afraid to impose, afraid we'll put her into a home. This is the last summer I'll spend like this.

August 27

Fran's gone back to work and put Celia into a residential home. Celia is totally different from Ma, but in the long run, does it matter? When we're old, we all need help. Fran says I'm too negative, that the home has planned activities and takes excellent care of the residents. Says her mom actually *likes* it. She thinks I'm "killing myself" because I can't stand up to Maury.

This is the only request he's asked of me. Fran will never understand that small voice in me that says, *This is my duty,* and an even smaller one that sometimes whispers, *I want to do this.* Still, I ask myself, does that voice come from me or from society?

August 29, Ashland, Oregon

In and out of the car, shoes on, shoes off, the dry heat keeping in all the odors of sweaty feet and leaking urine. Not one complaint; Ma's holding up marvelously.

Round One: Amy refuses to sleep in the same bed with Grandma. Her father is furious. I side with my kid—I've brought her up to be selfish. Can't expect her to accommodate now. Finally I say, "Go sleep outside in your sleeping bag." She does. Maury fumes. I want to kill him.

We're taking Ma to the Shakespeare Festival. Won't the family think well of us. Send them cards, show them we can do better than they can.

Amy: "Why couldn't Grandma stay home with Jon and Karen and Lori?"

Mom: "Because they're working and going to summer school; it's not fair to ask them. You know she's slow, she forgets to turn off the stove. They can't always be around if that happens."

Amy: "Why can't we be a normal American family?"

Mom (silently): Because what seems normal, isn't. This *is* normal.

September 1

Ma picks berries, a familiarity of childhood. She's ecstatic. Again, in and out of the car, to the toilet, to the gift shop, no we can't take a boat ride on Crater Lake, it's tiring for Grandma. Where's a chair for her?

Ma, are you sorry you came? No, better to come. How many more years to come?

Maury gives her his white cap; instant transformation. No more eastern European *babushka,* but a sporty West Coast Granny. All she needs is a pair of slacks. No, no, she laughs. She doesn't like her tush sticking out like an American girl.

We stop to eat. "My treat, from my money, take it from my account, Maury," she beams.

At the cabin she falls into bed but is up in half an hour. Maury touches me. I move away. "Are you upset?" he whispers.

"It doesn't matter," I lie.

In the middle of the night Ma calls out, "Am I in Saint Louis?"

Maury calls back, "No, Ma, you're with us on a vacation in Oregon. Good night."

September 7, Labor Day

Mission accomplished, well, partially. We took Ma on her first real American vacation. She even tried on an Elizabethan headdress. I saw lots of families with Grandmas, but it isn't working for me.

September 8

At the last minute, a part-time English job I applied for in March has come through! No, I didn't get hired for what I know, but for who I know. A social science instructor put in a good word for me. Maury says I'll be exploited as a part-timer. Maybe, but now that I have work, I feel better about Ma's stay here. With an early morning class at Jon's college, I can finish and get back home by 10:40 A.M. before Ma is even out of bed.

Time management is so important. Now I'll have some structure to my day. The kids promised they'd help in the morning if Grandma needs a hand, even Jon, provided I don't track him down and "bug" him on campus.

September 9

This afternoon I helped Ma look for the address of an old friend who had written her, the only letter she's received in months. It's as if Ma doesn't exist anymore. We opened her purse where she keeps obsolete invoices and old checking accounts, and sat on the bed thumbing through them. There were tears in her eyes. Too much a reminder of the past.

I searched around to see what else I could find. A picture of Pa. And there it is—her passport from 1923, with a picture of her I've never seen before. Such a young girl, not much older than my own daughters. A round, sweet face with large, sad eyes surprisingly resembling Karen.

September 10

Karen left yesterday. I can't believe it. Suddenly the house is so much larger—and so much emptier. Now we can play musical beds again.

September 11

Ma sitting in her chair engrossed in an old issue of *Newsweek*.

I'm amazed at her concentration. She hoists herself up and walks into the kitchen shaking the magazine in her hand.

"Here is bad news."

"What's happened?"

"The big rocket, the one they sent from Florida into the sky, it blew up. There were women inside. It had ice on it, and fire too. Now some little children will be without parents. The whole thing went kaput. You see, people cannot go ahead and act like God."

September 12

Ma and Amy are nursing TV. "Turn it down!" I yell.

Amy laughs. "Grandma's fun to watch with! She called Lucy 'stupid for marrying a crazy Cuban'!"

September 13

Ma in the yard. She looks around intensely at everything; she catches me checking on her, motions to me.

"Come, Claire, make a little time to sit here in this heaven with flowers, and look, a big mountain over there. You never sit outside."

"Yes, Ma, it's beautiful, but I've something to do now."

How different from her urban life. How rushed I am, escaping into my schoolwork.

September 14

Over four months since Ma's arrival. The whole family is talking about what a good son Maury is. They should see him put Ma to bed. I'm just the daughter-in-law who begrudgingly allows her to stay.

September 16

My class has started, and I'm enjoying it. Am looking forward to being away, earning some money, and having some sense of myself outside of this family. Ma wished me a belated good luck this morning.

"Don't worry, Claire darling. I take care of myself. Smiley and me will watch the house."

She should only know how much anxiety I have about leaving her alone three mornings a week.

September 18

Love being back in the classroom, having my mind on something solid. Hung around campus, ran errands, and didn't come home until 11:45 A.M., just in time to give Ma lunch. Four hours is a lot for her to be alone. Once out, I didn't want to go back, like a canary out of a cage.

September 19

Maybe I should take her out to lunch or to shop, but I so want my own free time.

September 20

I rage at myself for not talking to Helen when she called. Instead I nag Maury.

"Why can't she go back to Saint Louis for a few months? Why is having Ma easier for *me*? She can go to Saint Louis while it's still warm there and come back for the winter."

"Helen's too emotional. She remembers Ma as young, capable; she can't handle her."

"And I can?"

"You're not her daughter. You're a stronger person."

I lay on my bed thinking how I've never been real with Maury's family. And what do they care?

Bitterness only begets bitterness. I'll start a family rift I won't be able cope with.

October 6

Smiley is mopey today. Ma asks about him.

"The dog is sick?"

"Yes, Ma. I have to take him to the veterinarian."

"You pay this person?"

"Yes."

"I'll pay. I'll pay for the good dog. Go to my purse and write a check. Bring him back home in good health."

October 7

Since I've started teaching, I'm also tutoring in the Learning Center. I can separate myself from her more. Still, no matter how much she prefers to stay with us, no matter how much "Helen's afraid of handling her," she can't stay here indefinitely.

October 9

One of the teachers asked me if I want to join her for a weekend yoga retreat. I jumped at the chance. I'm leaving on Friday. I swear, I don't care what happens at home. At work I see the freedom other women have and realize how I've allowed this business to become all-consuming.

October 12

Returned from the retreat this morning. What a sense of well-being it gave me. I hadn't realized how tense I've been. Never even told Ma I was leaving. She thought I was "shopping" the whole time. Maury explained I'd been away.

"Away? Where does Claire go away all the time?"

Explain a yoga retreat to your mother-in-law. During the time I was there, I didn't think of her once. What I resent most isn't the physical work but the fact that I don't allow myself to do as I please.

October 15

A call from Helen. Maury was out; otherwise, she'd never speak to me about Ma's financial status.

Amazing how civil we are, how I control my anger the moment I hear her voice, how we "befriend one another," play the roles of "two women against Maury." Politely I ask if it's "possible" for her to take Ma over the summer. Politely she answers, "I'll think it over. Barney's not feeling well right now."

October 19

Ma lying in bed deathly quiet. I come in to straighten her pillow.

"Claire?"

"Yes, Ma?"

"I had a dream. My mother. Her face was nice and pink. She wore her long blue dress and her *shabbas* wig. She knows I'm sick. 'Hildy, you are my favorite. Eat this and you will be strong.' She blessed me. 'Take care of yourself,' she says. She gave me the same honey candies she cooked in a pot when I was a girl. She's trying to help me. Her cheeks were pink the way I remember."

An hour later Ma gets out of bed and walks into the pantry thinking it's the bathroom. She stands there helplessly until I lead her back to her room. After another half an hour, she calls, "Claire darling, do you have some *cholent?*"

"No, I don't cook *cholent*. Would you like tea and toast?"

No answer. I walk into her room. She's vomited all over herself. She grasps my arm, hangs onto it, says it's *finster*, dark, while the sun is streaming in. Then she says something she's never said before. "Claire darling, I feel afraid. Stay with me a few minutes."

I sit with her until she falls into a peaceful sleep.

Maury's so worried, he talks about buying a casket and making funeral and burial arrangements out here.

"What's the sense of shipping her body back?" he asks.

"But she always said she wanted to be buried next to your dad, didn't she?"

He doesn't answer.

October 21

Ma is very ill. She cannot leave now. Although she's not paralyzed, it might be a partial stroke. She cried out in her nap, but later made an effort to joke.

"Like a drunkard I am. Like a bottle of schnapps I drank up. A shikker who doesn't know where to walk." She laughed, her eyes tearful.

Maury's calm; in fact, he thought she could shower alone, but I was too worried. For the first time in months, I helped her bathe. Lori gave me a hand. Such a strong, confident girl. She practically carried Ma out of the tub. Ma looked up at her and gratefully said, "You saved my life, you good girl."

October 24

Every woman has the right to die the way she wants. Maybe she'll die of a broken heart. But why so negative? She'll get better in a few days. Maury's taking her to the doctor.

October 26

Must get help in the house. I've already missed a week of school. This morning Maury went to work late so I could get home from my class before he left.

October 27

The doctor doesn't think Ma had a stroke but has an unpredictable "vascular disorder" that will take six to eight weeks to clear up. Says it's difficult to diagnose older patients; sometimes they have small strokes no one knows about, even themselves. He tells us not to worry.

Maury announces, "On the days Claire teaches, we'll have a woman here to help you so you won't be alone."

"I'm good like new. I don't need no one. I take care of myself. Save the money for the kids."

I want to yell, "Don't make it hard for me; it's already hard enough," but restrain myself.

Later, on our walk, I tell Maury how I feel.

"Can you really get angry with an old woman who's confused and sick?"

Okay, darling, I'll stuff my mouth with silence; I'll transfer my anger to you.

October 29

> *Night rain sinks into the soil / you sink into me / night / at last she*
> *sleeps / there is no dichotomy of body and mind / oh yes, my love,*
> *I say / she will not separate us / till the light of day / this is my*
> *time to be alone with you / you must understand how hard it is /*

to hang on to all my pieces / who would believe a simple old good
woman could drive us apart / why can't you be like other men /
why must you care so much / is this my reason for loving you

October 30

Shocked this morning when Ma put on all of her clothes backward. Said she couldn't see. She's disoriented, can't find her way from the bedroom to the bathroom. I've been crying all day. What an emotional roller coaster.

November 1

To the doctor again. He confirmed the fact that she's had a small stroke, accompanied by "a slight loss of vision"—some of it will return in about a month.

Of all things! I've dreamt of her falling, breaking bones, having a heart attack. But not her eyes. Her reading and sewing are the last things she had.

November 2

Dr. Merkel told us Ma could have an operation to prevent further strokes. Maury doesn't buy it, thinks she's too old.

"Why did you wait over a week to phone Helen and Arnold?" I demand.

"I don't want to alarm them; I wanted to be exactly sure of her condition first."

No comment. Ma traveling is out of the question for now.

Feel a rage to live, to do everything I've ever wanted. I listened to Vivaldi's *Four Seasons* with intense passion tonight.

November 3

Today's paper: an eighty-one-year-old woman dies from a mugging. Sick society we live in. Sick, and I, too, a part of this sickness. Didn't give Ma her lunch until after 1:00 because I didn't want to deal with her. Finally I called her.

"Ma, aren't you hungry? It's almost 1:30 P.M."

"Yes, I am very hungry, Claire darling; I've been hungry for a long time."

"Why didn't you tell me? I could have made lunch earlier."

"You were busy at your desk."

Sick.

November 4

Karen calls from school, and I tell her about Ma. She listens for a few minutes and says, "Be patient, Mom."

November 5

We've started to use a bedpan. She's in bed a lot, and I can't carry her to the bathroom. The other day she got stuck on the toilet; I had to call a neighbor to help me lift her and steer her back to bed.

Maury's bought a small commode. Wonder if I'll ever get used to it. Right now I hate it.

November 6

Jon moved out. He and Linda took an apartment in the city. He was never home anyway. Can't blame him, but he's so young, it bothers me. I'll have to get used to a kid of nineteen living with his girlfriend in San Francisco. Linda's parents don't like the idea either.

November 7

Dora Roberts came to help Ma today. At first I resented having anyone at all.

Dora is a deeply religious person, full of kindness. She's been praying all day. Ma liked the attention and told her, "Darling, I'm glad you come to help me."

Dora sat with Ma in the sun talking, then led her about for a few steps, gave her lunch. After lunch she gave Ma a bath. She'll be coming three mornings a week. Overheard Ma tell her about Maury, "My son is good. He asks me to stay here. He thinks of others."

"Lord, oh Lord, bless some good menfolks," Dora chuckled.

She suggested we rent a wheelchair so she can take Ma around the block for a change of scenery. Every new apparatus is another reminder of Ma's debilitation, but it makes life easier.

November 9

When Dora walks in at 7:00 A.M., I walk out. Could leave later, but I don't have enough to do here and am uncomfortable delegating responsibility. Then I rush back from school just in time to let her go.

"It could have been worse, Ma," I say. "You're going to get better."

"God watches me," she wisely nods.

Told Maury Ma can stay until she fully recuperates, but then she's got to go to Helen.

"And what if she doesn't recuperate?"

Hadn't thought of that.

November 10

Exercised in aerobics with uncommon energy this morning. With every bend and twist I could smell her presence, her clothes. Beneath the sound of that screaming music swam her face, her left eye small and dry looking. Have been consumed with "Claire's rage to live." Looked at every man on the way home.

November 13

We've finally reorganized. Amy is sharing Lori's and Karen's old room. Jon is busy with his own life. He spends more time with Linda's family than ours.

Meanwhile, Maury has mailed away for a special tape recorder and tapes in Yiddish that Ma can listen to now that she can't read. And me, I just wait to see what will happen.

November 14

No further expectations, no more hope that she'll fold laundry or wash a dish again. In a way her illness makes things easier. At last I accept her doing nothing. Fran says I should have moved her into an apartment with a housekeeper. She calls Maury a "benevolent tyrant" and, of course, thinks I'm a fool.

November 16

My mother calls to ask about Hilda, how she's recuperating from her stroke. "How horrible. How shocking."

"Mother, for an old woman, she's doing pretty well. You have to expect things like this. She doesn't complain."

"How's Maury taking it?"

"He's not a child. It's not the end of the world."

"Claire, I'm surprised at you. Do you think she got ill because she knows she has to leave you?"

"Please don't mention that."

I hang up irritated with Mom for making too much of Ma's stroke. Old people have strokes.

Then why am I upset when my neighbor doesn't ask how she is, and why do I start to cry when I hear Ma's broken voice in her room, Dora consoling her.

November 17

She sits at the table, sulks, barely touches her food, has become demanding. "Claire, bring me a napkin. Claire, take this plate away."

Remind myself it's not yet four weeks since her stroke. Her walking is still shaky. Better that she's here with us than back East at Helen's, where she wouldn't be able to walk the stairs.

Lori and Amy have been great about helping her to the toilet. I do what I have to, no more—don't sit around holding her hand. When I leave the house, I put her in bed. This business of getting her to the toilet remains troublesome. We have to start using that damn commode.

November 20

Though Ma complains, "I don't need a baby-sitter," she's listless without Dora. If I manage to be productive by ignoring her, I feel dehumanized— like one of those highly achieving women who accomplishes her goal by caring nothing for others, one who constantly escapes her family responsibilities. I've never appreciated women like that.

November 22

Helen calls Maury to ask about Ma. She says it right out loud. "I won't be able to take her this spring. It's too much for me. I've got my own problems here; you know Barney isn't well. It's too much with his illness. Can't you put her into a nursing home? It would be the best thing for all of us."

Nearly went mad listening on the extension.

Maury's voice grows quiet. He parrots her words. "Yes, it's too much with Barney's illness."

The dam bursts. I fly into a rage and slam down the bedroom phone. I run into the kitchen. "What's the matter with you? You both promised. *Say something!*"

He covers the mouthpiece so Helen won't hear. He hangs up, stands there, immobilized. "I can't believe it. I simply can't believe it."

"What do mean, you can't believe it? Give me that phone. I'm calling her back this instant."

"*Don't.* Can't you accept her limitations? If she can't do it, you can't force her. Why take your aggression out on her? She feels guilty enough."

The veins in my temples pound with all my years of repressed feelings about both his behavior with his family and my own. I block out Barney and everyone else and dial her number.

"Helen, this may be the last time we ever speak. It's your obligation to take Ma for three months. You promised me back in August."

"I never promised. I said I would see. I didn't know she'd have a stroke and that Barney would take so long to recuperate."

Silence. Then I hear weeping, then, "Okay, Claire, okay." She hangs up.

A few minutes later Mary Alice phones. She's venomous.

"Helen won't do it. *I'll* take Ma in the spring."

I gulp hard. "Okay, I can wait until spring."

"But I'm going to fix Helen. She won't step a foot into my house to see her mother, Claire."

I want to say something, but don't. Finally, "That's between the two of you." I hang up.

Maury lies down in bed and cries.

November 24

Thanksgiving is in two days; for the sake of the kids we do not argue. We will have no guests, just our family, minus Jon. He'll be with Linda. We must not show the kids this rift that's grown between us.

November 25

How and when did all this begin? You weren't like this when we first married. You were never tied to her. Didn't we leave her to come to California? Didn't we take vacations?

If one more woman tells me how "feeling" you are, I'll tear out my hair. Let her try living with you 5,000 days and see what happens.

so white you are waiting / waiting for death / so silent you are /
not a word not a thought / waiting / not fearing the vast silence /
the soul crying out in that vastness / was there a time / when the
walls of your village / didn't sing / or sigh / with the full goodness
of you / when your hair was black / before America when you
rode the ocean / rode the waves / stars in the nebulae / across this
table from me / this morning / this late Thanksgiving in your life

November 27

Except for her complaints of dizziness, Ma's doing better. She recognizes things and certainly sees large objects. This morning Maury actually took her to synagogue for an hour. At first she refused to go.

"No, let people feel sorry for themselves, not for me because I don't see good."

Amy counters with, "You're not going for people, Grandma. Did you ever see God when your eyes were okay?"

A weak laugh. "No."

"Then maybe you'll see Him now that your eyes are weaker!"

After they left, Lori said, "I swear Dad will die before Grandma the way he's been acting lately."

November 28

What if Barney is sicker than I think? Am I losing all sense of perspective?

November 30

Dora gave me an extra day today. She's good with Ma, but her praying can be hard to take.

December 1

Maury's ordered Ma a special handmade pair of shoes for four hundred dollars. Her feet have been killing her from her bunions. I doubt if she'll ever wear them.

December 3

Oh beast, be tamed. An evening out for myself. Listening to Rabbi Leibman, a rare man of wisdom. The path is what counts: that path for me right now is to accept my husband's mother in our home, not to involve myself with all kinds of outside "causes."

The rage is silent for tonight.

December 5

While I was gone for a few hours, the kids forgot to give Grandma lunch.

"She didn't ask for it," Lori defended herself.

Jon, who was visiting, yelled, "Yeah, you should know; you're the one who said her breath was awful when she was in the kitchen!"

"You could have done it! You don't think you have to help with Grandma just because you don't live here anymore!" She banged the door and rode out on her bike in the rain.

I gritted my teeth. "Looks like Grandma caught a cold, too. Her nose is red. Did you let her sit in the yard this morning without a sweater?"

"Don't bug us, she's not our problem!" Amy shouted. "She left her snot rags in our bedroom while she was going through our stuff."

"She's bored, that's why," I say with a weak shrug.

December 7

Ma had her tooth pulled today; it was hanging by a hair. She worried our dentist might charge too much. Mumbling, she reverted to Yiddish, "Does he know I'm a landlady? Dentists can be gonifs."

"No, Ma, he doesn't know, and this dentist isn't a thief."

No need to remind her the building's been sold and the assets transferred to an account to pay for her care—when the time comes.

She put on such heavy cologne that when she walked into the waiting room a patient asked, "What smells of Christmas trees?"

After Ma relaxed she sat in the dentist's chair looking pale and innocent. She thanked Dr. Fong, and pecked him on the cheek. "God bless you, my son." He turned pale.

December 8

Sophie, one of the women I drive to the JCC, has been lecturing her divorced daughter on my "sainthood." Apparently Andrea insists that her mother live alone.

Sophie invites both of us to lunch, then pits Andrea against me.

"See this nice woman? The same age as you. Four children, two more than you, and now her husband's mother lives with her, too. Not like you."

Immediately Andrea becomes my "enemy."

"I don't know your friend, Mother, but she's married, and I'm not. I'm sure she has enough leisure time and money to do whatever she wants. She doesn't have to work like I do."

The two of them continue to discuss me in the third person as if I'm not there. I don't bother explaining myself; instead, I stare at the wall.

"That's not the point; the point is she makes time for—"

"Mother, please, I'm a professional woman. And I need time for some social life."

"And you don't want me around."

"Come off it! Did you ever support anything I wanted to do when I was a kid?"

"How can you talk about what happened thirty years ago? Don't you have any sense of responsibility?"

I felt so used; I stood up and excused myself. How deep these old wounds. Made me seriously think that I'd never want to live with any of my own kids. Whose drummer could I march to—Amy's?

The lunch didn't change Andrea's mind one bit. At first I liked her direct-ness—until she began making assumptions about me. Too bad people don't see the situation in its entirety.

December 9

Dream: I'm in some kind of women's brainwashing camp because I'm female. Invisible electrodes are plugged into my body, which is divided into a grid. All the women are separated into three groups. I'm in the third group. Neither clothed nor unclothed, our bodies are blank paper dolls without organs or genitals. The electrodes are plugged into the right side of my body. When my turn for interro-gation comes, I'm not sure if I should try to break out of the mold I'm "plugged" into. Silently, I tell myself, "Try, at least make an effort. You can do it." As I'm called before the Grand Inquisitor to say the words "honor and duty," I repeat them in front of a giant screen, but don't mean them and utter to myself, "No one can take my thoughts away." Immediately, a buzz goes off all over the left side of my body, and the Inquisitor knows.

Couldn't shake these images for a long time when I woke this morning. Scary. Think I know what they mean.

December 14

How quietly she rests in her chair waiting for Dora. If only I could rest like that. If only I could trust like that. Blessed be old women, be they black, white, or yellow, who take care of other old women, who change their sheets and do not hate them, who accept their age and do not fear it.

Am I jealous of Dora, of her ability to work with Ma? That she can sit outside in the yard with Ma in peace while I pace about, prisoner in my own house? I close my bedroom door and throw myself into grading finals.

December 16

Why do I keep putting it off? Dora can't give me any more hours. Unless I let her go and find someone full-time, I've got to hire another woman on the days Dora's not here. How will I ever get used to *two* women?

December 17

I won't be the one responsible for placing her in a nursing home. With added help, maybe we can delay it, but even if Ma goes to Mary Alice for a few months, commuting back and forth can't work forever.

December 19

Maury calls Arnie to talk about Ma. He puts her on for a few minutes. I stand in the hallway and listen: "Yes, Arnold darling, fine. Maury and Claire are good to me. Don't worry."

Don't worry. My stomach churns.

After Maury hangs up, we get into a row over his family.

"He has more compassion than you think."

"What good is it if he won't help out?"

"He couldn't do a good job even if he tried."

"I bet he had the nerve to ask her how we're treating her."

"You're getting so worked up, the next thing you know, you'll be taking out your anger about him on her."

"What? I've never hurt your mother. Is that what you think of me?"

"You don't realize it. She already senses nobody wants her."

"Is that my fault? A woman at school told me her mother wouldn't dream of *imposing* by moving in, that's what she said!"

I will not bend to his will. I will not take on Maury's role with his mother. I have my own life to live.

December 20

The fifth day of Chanukah. We heat up a few leftover *latkes*. Maury puts on a record and helps Ma light the menorah. Her blessing is always the same—"We should all live together to another year in good health"—and for a moment, I find myself embracing her. Jon, who rushed in to see us for fifteen minutes, "dances" with her in her chair. Then he rushes out.

After we finish, Ma sneaks back into the kitchen and grabs some rendered chicken skins I was going to throw out, *gribbiness,* and hides them in the pocket of her flowered nightgown. She knows how I feel about her eating pure fat. Quietly, she hobbles back down the hall to her room, smacking her lips and muttering, "I got everything I need."

December 21

Karen is home for the holidays; she has nowhere to put her clothes. Ma starts telling her about the building she owned. "Beautiful flats they are. I keep them up. I rent to good paying people, no bums. Reasonable. You can't get places like that."

Karen blushes, "But Grandma, Dad's already sold the building." Ma walks out of the room in dead silence.

December 22

Get dressed early for your Chanukah party Ma; sit in the chair all morning and wait for the senior bus to drive you to the JCC. This time I'm stubborn and won't drive. How timidly you'll enter the room. Nowhere to sit: those big old babies saving places for their friends; see how they carefully place napkins on the nearest chair. You'll have to sit next to that old man you don't like. You don't like menfolk now. Too many years of waiting on them. Put in your teeth. Smooth down your hair. Sing aloud, eyes shining, *"Chanukah, oh, Chanukah, yontif and fraylich."* Where are your teeth? You've left them behind.

December 23

We all go to the Good Earth in Berkeley for an early dinner for our anniversary. Linda comes too. Ma sits in her chair waiting for hours so she'll "be ready for Mauryle." Lori and Karen put so much rouge on her that she looks like one of those Russian nesting dolls. She refuses the food on the menu because it "costs too much."

"We eat better at home," she says in a loud voice. "Look at this lettuce. Already wilted."

Embarrassed, Linda and Jon decide to sit at a separate table by themselves. We all pretend we're having a great time.

December 28

Not sure, but it seems Ma has regained most of her sight. We've started to bring large-print books into the house. And Maury's ordered free tapes from the braille society. At first the droning of the music and stories irritated me, but now she uses Jon's old headphones. She gets a lot of pleasure from listening. Maury says when she dies the best way to remember her is with a contribution to the braille organization.

December 30

Still haven't found anyone to replace Dora. The first woman I interviewed gave a reference that accused her of child abuse, the second one was so hostile, I felt intimidated. This process is harder than I thought—and more expensive. How I hate having anyone here at all, but there's no alternative….God, sometimes I wish I were Superwoman.

1988

Claire is not a good girl

January 2, 1988

> *fill me with ease / so my limbs live / and my heart hears its beat /*
> *how I've betrayed myself / running from you / how I want to free*
> *myself / but in my flight / I find no pleasure / nor purity of vision /*
> *only that part / of me / which is you*

January 3

We've found someone to come in five days a week from eight till four.
Felt terrible letting Dora go. So far Ma doesn't like Anna, starts screaming
when she arrives, "*Oy*, I'm dying, I'm dying. You, lady, don't touch me."

Anna's just arrived from the Philippines; does she see Ma as another old
white woman in a wasting body? When I showed her an early picture of
Ma, she shook her head wondrously. We both stood in the hallway
looking at that snapshot for a long time.

January 6

Today Anna came so late I couldn't go to winter orientation for classes.
Afraid to leave Ma alone even for two hours. Maury said she'd be okay,
but if something happens, I think it will be my fault.

Anna seems to like us and wants to make a "deal": since her agency
deducts half of her wages, she'll quit them and come to work for us on
her own *if* we hire her full-time. Never thought I'd be embroiled in
domestic help problems.

January 8

At dinner Maury and I talk about a weekend break and asking Anna to
stay over. Even he admits we need some time alone. Amy had a fit.

"It's not fair to leave me here with Grandma and her nurses!"

Sorry, Amy, it's time for Dad and me to spend one night alone.

January 11

Anna: Hilda, she was sick while you are away. I had to sleep in her room all night. The kids stay out very late. I like Hilda. She is easy to take care of, a nice woman—good—but when I was sleeping with her in her room, a bad thing happened. I start to get old—very, very old. I will take care of her during the day, but I cannot stay at night again.

January 12

> *warts pop from my nose / nails grow long and lethal / curses fall from cupboards / a pox on order / a plague on neatness / all day I stir my brew / waiting for night to transform these words to my will / even love / won't stop me now*

January 13

"Good morning, Ma. Are you ready for your breakfast?"

"No, darling. Is that nice black lady coming today?"

"No, Ma, she quit. Anna's supposed to come; she's late."

"The young one who talks too much?"

"I thought you like to watch 'I Love Lucy' with her."

Silence. So be it. As soon as Anna arrives, off to my room to dress for class, the sound of voices drifting through my door.

January 15

This morning Ma shit all over herself. I spent an hour cleaning up the bathroom. Clean up the shit, Claire. Have you forgotten when the kids were babies? Today Ma's an old powerless woman who can't control her bowels. How that powerlessness manifests itself into our lives!

Amy comes into the bathroom to watch me.

"Get out of here!" I shout, not wanting her to see the mess.

"Boy, you're a crab! No wonder Dad talks to Grandma at dinner and not you. *She* always smiles and listens."

"Yeah?" I yell from the bathroom floor. "I wish Grandma would croak!"

"Mom! You're awful!"

The words just slipped out of me, the way the shit slipped out of Ma and onto the floor.

January 16

After yesterday's incident, I've decided to use the money I earn to see a therapist. Was able to get a last minute cancellation this morning with Susan Cole. She tells me my feelings of anger and guilt toward Ma are related to my own lack of fulfillment and self-worth. There's something to this, but how can I change? It will take a lifetime.

January 23

Susan suggests that I join a support group for people with problems of aging parents. She says my difficulties are common for "women in the middle years," and unless I'm willing to spend a lot of time discussing my own parents and background, I'd be wasting money on private therapy.

She's right. I *don't* want to discuss my childhood with Mom and Dad—even if it does relate to how I handle Ma. Just want to take care of what upsets me now.

January 24

Lori: "Grandma, turn the light on; it's too dark for you to read."

"I'm not reading. I like sitting in darkness."

"What are you doing?"

"Thinking. I tell my eyes, 'Eyes you have been good to me and last a long time. Please last a little longer.' But they say they must rest now. So I listen to them."

"Grandma!"

"It's true, darling," she smiles.

January 28

Maury has purchased a huge contraption called a Hoyer Lift, a swing-like apparatus on chrome poles, to help Ma with her bath. Anna places her in the seat and cranks it up to lift her into the tub. Ma hates it. Don't know how Anna manages to get her into it. With all her medicines, her commode, and this new apparatus, our house feels like it's turning into a nursing home.

January 29

Asked Ma to help with the dishes so she'd feel useful—not an impossible task for her. Maury grabbed the plate out of her hand.

"She's not your maid. Let her rest."

"She rested all day. It's good for her to do something."

"She's not washing greasy pots because *you* don't like to do them."

I threw down the sponge in disgust. "You're a damn fool!"

Ma grew frightened. "Don't be like that, Maury darling. Claire is a good girl."

"Claire is *not* a good girl!" I yell.

Ma looked stunned. "I never talked like this to my husband's mother."

I go to bed dreaming of murder and divorce. I'd love to take that university extension class that's being offered in Paris and leave everyone behind.

February 6

"He was a perfect baby. The others wouldn't eat. Arnold throwing down his botty, Helen crying all night. But not Maury. He loved his botty. That's why his teeth are good. That's why your children's teeth are beautiful, yes, Claire?"

"What? Yes, Ma. Excuse me, I have to grade papers." I slink off to look at a postcard a friend sent me from a week-long conference on women and politics. Seems like no one else has old relatives to take care of but me. So many of my friends have broken off with family to pursue their own lives.

February 10

Ma at breakfast without her teeth, her head hunched between her shoulders, studying her bowl lovingly. Eating from the pot so as not to "spoil a dish," grabbing the cooked prunes, throwing everything onto Maury's plate. I get up from the table and leave the two of them sitting there.

February 13

Saturday. Maury sits in the kitchen coaxing Ma to write a letter to Arnold. Her writing is shaky but she manages:

> *Dear Arnold and Mary Alice,*
>
> *I am fine with Maury and Claire and their good children. They have a nice house and are good to me. I like it here. I go to the JCC for lunch sometimes. It is not cold in February.*
>
> *Your Loving Mother, Hilda*

I look at Maury. "Aren't you going to add anything about her visit this spring? It'll be a year that she's been here by then."

"Not this time. Let's wait."

Does he know some dark secret about his family I don't?

Before I can ask, the kids bounce in with their antics and make Grandma laugh. "Lori darling, you're so pretty, some hot guy is going to grab you up."

Everyone admires the letter Grandma's managed to write—but me.

February 25

Today during Jon's visit, Grandma finally realized that he's not living here any longer.

"Linda and I took an apartment together," he explains with pride.

Her response, "Why not?"

Delighted with her, Jon took Ma in his arms—she comes up to his waist—and danced a gentle little hora with her until she was out of breath.

"See how kind and understanding she is, Mom? Why aren't you like that?"

"Sometimes Grandma's judgment is off."

"Mom, not in front of her!"

He was more attentive to her than usual, brought her tooth powder for her dentures before she went to bed. He hates when she walks around without her teeth, but tonight he was on her side.

March 1

Spring's around the corner. When are we going to set a date for Ma's flight?

"Wouldn't you like to visit Arnold for a while?"

"How will I get there?"

"By plane. Maury will fly with you, the way he brought you here."

"To Poland?"

"No, Ma, to Saint Louis, to see Helen and Arnold."

"It is better for me here. I like it here."

March 2

Amy: "After Grandpa Sam died, did you ever like any other men?"

"No, darling, but one liked me."

"But you didn't like him?"

"I'm not the type like some of my old widow friends who doll up and run around."

"But what if you, say, *did* love him?"

"Love is hot when you're young, darling, but this grandma, she didn't want to take care of menfolks; they're too much trouble. I had other things to do. Besides, I got a good family, and all my money is for them, not old *boychiks*."

March 3

A social protester of seventy doesn't just suddenly become a social protester. The seeds are planted early in life. A bitter, helpless woman of seventy plants her seeds early, too. Still, there's no guarantee for the way anyone ages. Must start thinking of what I want to do in the coming decades, plan for them—to follow the examples of women who are involved with society, not sit back and wait for the optimum moment. It may never come.

March 4

To the dentist again. Ma sits like a sphinx. Yes, Ms. Receptionist, we can pay. Don't give me that look; you know she's not a welfare patient.

On the way out we meet an old acquaintance of Ma's, Rose Blumenthal. Ma is standing in the hallway, cotton stuffed in her mouth, her jaw swollen, unable to talk, when Mrs. Blumenthal, still hardy, runs over to us.

"It's Hilda, Hilda Brenner. My God, I don't know you. What's happened?"

She's not just referring to the fact that Ma had one of her last teeth pulled out.

We chat for a moment and learn that Mrs. Blumenthal's unmarried niece has invited her to live out here in an apartment in the same complex.

At dinnertime I tell Maury we met an old friend of Ma's. He's delighted. "Isn't it nice to meet someone you know? You can invite Rose over."

"I don't want her. You and Claire and the kids are enough."

"But you always liked her. Don't you want to know how she got here and where she's living?"

"Here is here; there is there. She's a nudnik, she knows everyone's business."

"Did you ask her where she lives?"

"No. Now I go to bed." And she walks out of the kitchen.

March 5

Tomorrow night I'm going to a support group for adults of elderly disabled parents.

March 6, Support Group

Tonight we discussed the pros and cons of nursing homes. Then someone told horror stories about a scandal—some phony cure for removing aluminum from the brain of Alzheimer's patients.

The facilitator led us away from general complaints; she wanted specifics.

She opened up a tinderbox. Everyone began talking at once.

"My mother's hyperventilating, and I'm starting to do the same when I visit her."

"I hate my wife for making me her mother's caretaker!"

"When my dad goes, we'll celebrate. I can't take it anymore!"

And a Russian woman learning English cried, "And I hate my mother for stopping the walking and to starting the crawl on the floor, a baby! What will happen when we too are old?"

Facilitator: "Friends, friends, slow down; remember, these incidents represent only 5 percent of the elderly who become incapacitated. *You* may not. Many old people live rich and full lives."

March 9

Time is coming closer. I can hear them now:

Arnold: "She sends me these stupid notes. What does she want? Maury does everything anyway. Always was a women's libber. Who wouldn't love Ma? Just put her in a chair; she doesn't ask for anything. She better stop bugging Mary Alice. We have a new baby to take care of, and I'm not ruining this marriage."

Helen: "I did my share. I took care of her for years after Pa died, visited every weekend, had her every holiday. Claire with her nasty letters and holier-than-thou attitude—what does she know?"

March 13, Support Group

Jill: "Mom's fine until I come to visit. Then she gets 'sick.' I lie to her, tell her I'm still working, because if she knew I'd been laid off, she'd call me a million times."

Claire: "I lie too. I tell Ma I'm teaching all day when I really finish at noon. That way I justify staying away until three."

Jill: "When Mom comes over, I'm able to get her to do some sewing."

Claire: "I've stopped trying. I wish I could find something that Maury's mother would do. She's going downhill."

Facilitator: "It's not your responsibility to keep her alert, Claire. Your responsibility is to protect her, but you can't keep her from growing senile."

Claire (defensive): "Senile?" We've never used *that* word for her before. "Really, she's not senile."

Facilitator: "You must learn to accept her limitations and your own or you won't be able to deal with her. All you'll do is increase your stress level."

March 17

Smiley died today. He was nearly fourteen. The kids have been crying all day. Ma seems sad too. "Dogs, they have a soul too, don't they, Claire darling?"

Yes, Ma, yes.

A few neighbors sent us cards, one small girl even brought us a plate of cookies. Seems like our old dog was more valuable in this community than our Grandma who barely has any visitors at all. Certainly no one who brings her cookies.

March 20, Support Group

Edith: "After all I've done for my father, he accuses me of stealing. He doesn't remember where he's invested his money, repeats over and over again the same questions about his bills, then blames me for ripping him off."

Facilitator: "There's a difference between asking for attention and truly not remembering. Are you sure he doesn't remember?"

Edith: "I'm sure. I hate to say this, the idea sickens me, but I may have to declare him incompetent."

Facilitator: "He'll need an evaluation by a psychologist and a social worker. Are you familiar with Durable Power of Attorney? It allows you to become the trustee of his estate."

Edith: "He'll never agree to that."

Facilitator: "If two medical people concur, it's possible. And now that Edith has had this experience, all of you should also acquaint yourselves with annuity insurance to protect yourselves."

Edith (covers her face with her hands): "On top of that, he and my son band together to make me the common enemy."

She begins to sob. Our facilitator reaches out to console her.

Can all this be happening? Sounds like a soap opera, the cruel parent and grandchild ganging up against the middle-aged child. Boy, I'm lucky not to have to cope with anything like this.

March 21

Ma goes into the backyard, lifts her skirt, and pees in nearly the same spot that Smiley used, as if that act connects her with our old dog.

March 22

"Guess who I met shopping today? Mrs. Blumenthal with her niece. They want to visit you."

"No, Rose Blumenthal is a dumbbell and a *yenta*. I don't need her to feel sorry for me."

Lori yells out, laughing from her room. "That a girl, Grandma, you always tell the truth."

I myself chuckle sadly. She still knows her own mind.

March 24

Four-thirty A.M. Rustling in the kitchen. Ma standing in the dark, peeking out the window. Lori's voice: "But Gram, it's too early. I'll take you back to your room."

"I was waiting for Daddy. I thought I was going to the JCC. Is it time for dinner? Maybe Mamma's got a piece of salami with mustard and pickle."

Lori laughs, "Are you kidding? She doesn't bring that stuff into the house. If I want some, I buy it and eat it in the deli."

"Too bad. Mamma's missing something. A little salami never hurt anyone."

March 26

A letter from Mary Alice! She promises to take Ma for six weeks this summer! I'd hoped for three or four months, but at this point, I'm glad for anything. As soon as Mary Alice is back from her vacation, I'll look for flights. Hard to break the news. Better to wait or prepare Ma now?

Maybe Mary Alice doesn't handle Ma the way Maury likes, but she *has* recuperated, and it *is* possible to work with her at home. People *can* care for members at home—if they want to.

March 27, Support Group

"In our tradition, we stay with the body after it is no longer alive; we try to hold onto it. Back in Mexico we have *Dia de los Muertos* to help us; *tambien* in villages we keep the dead in our house. We light candles; we sit with the body. Here the health law say no. There our children eat *pan de muertos* and little sugar skeletons."

An overwhelming silence.

Then, "When my father died, I said kaddish for him. It helped me to separate myself from him. To know he was in a place where I couldn't go. I was able to give away all his clothes and his car three weeks after he was gone."

More silence. Three weeks! I couldn't believe it. Don't think it would be possible for me. I have so little experience with dying; I want to learn about death rites at other times and in other cultures.

Only two more meetings, and this session ends.

March 30

"Don't make her go, Claire. It's not a good idea. I promise I'll make it up to you later. She'll be in Arnold's basement by herself. She fell last time. Mary Alice means well, but she doesn't know how to care for her."

I turn away. "Leave me alone."

Ma walks to the pantry, gets a shopping bag and comes into the living room. "Don't fight, children. We'll go in the car to Helen's now."

Maury walks her back to her room. I lock myself in the bathroom.

He bangs on the door. "I'll call Helen tomorrow; I'll ask her once more."

April 3, Support Group

Quiet tonight at support group. Didn't feel like contributing. Our facilitator identified four kinds of caregivers, mentioning that for some of them—*us*, why is it so hard for me to use that word?—the stress level becomes so high it raises the blood pressure and causes changes in the immune system; yet a few—*of course Maury*—thrive on caring for their charge. Well, I'm not him.

Later, Tina talked about how her mother didn't know her dad had died, and still addressed her as "Little Tina" as if her mom were in a time warp. The woman didn't do that with Tina's sister, Beverly, who is thirteen years older. "Beverly thinks it's funny, but I get mad."

Hmm.

Some talk about not medicating patients if it makes them more cognizant but also agitated. What's better? A more aware old charge and more nervous caregiver, or a less aware charge and a less nervous caregiver?

I didn't want to be present tonight, maybe because I don't have the answers. Felt like forgetting the whole business and—what?—escaping to the moon.

April 4

The left burner on the stove is smoking. Three dishes crash to the floor. Ma stands in the kitchen looking helpless.

"I wanted, Claire darling, to help, make things easier for you. I tried to cook for you. Maybe I didn't see too good." She weeps as I lead her back to her room.

How many times I too have been forgetful, left the stove on myself. Cursed be age, cursed be the loss of one's abilities.

April 8

Dream: I kill someone. It is the kind old queen. I kill her because I don't want to see her feed her grown son breakfast at my table. I cannot find my freedom with her surrounding me. I will never find my freedom. I cut my hands that act in evil without my will but of their own. I cut a slice of darkness and wrap it around myself, a shawl, a cloak—my poverty/charity/chastity. I'm a beggar woman for the rest of my life. I beg in villages only a bowl of milk, a crust of bread. I keep nothing for myself.

April 10, Support Group

For our final meeting, our facilitator called in a specialist to tell us about hospices. In the bathroom during the break, Kimberly said under her breath, "You know, you can only go there if you promise to die in three weeks." I appreciated her black humor.

Apparently, the big question is: When do you send a dying person to a hospice, and what if the entire family won't agree? The first part of the question has an answer: When the patient has been at home and can no longer eat. The second part is more difficult.

The last twenty minutes we had a "party" and socialized. No talk about illness was allowed, only talk about what "goodies" we were planning for ourselves. Still, one of the men wanted to ask questions about the Hemlock Society and what it entails. The group's been beneficial, but, hell, I don't wanna be part of it anymore! Even though new topics will be discussed, I'm not taking the next session.

April 16

Arnold "forbids" Mary Alice to take Ma. He says her presence will jeopardize their marriage. What about *my* marriage, what about *my* life?

April 17

My friends were right. I didn't understand what was in store when Ma came here to live. I didn't define limits. I needed to be the "good" one, to play that role as much as I denied it in myself, had to show others the "Certificate of Appreciation" for driving seniors.

April 20

Shaky. For the first time I say it openly. "If your mother doesn't go to your brother's or sister's this summer, then she's going to a nursing home."

"Do you mean it?"

"She goes or I go."

Maury bangs the table. "Then go. I'll never put her into a home. She's not going to die like my grandmother did. I'll leave here before I do that. I'll get a place for both of us." And then a deep bursting sound, "I'll look for something tomorrow."

What have I done?

April 23

> *He had to have his mother / it was his duty / the wife allowed it: /*
> *"Do not desert me in my old age." / Still she raged at the old*
> *woman's goodness / she was close to leaving / he too looked at ads*

for a place to stay with Mother / the house / the bills / where
would it lead / She turned against Mother / him / still she didn't
leave / he didn't leave / they weren't that kind of couple

April 26

More calls.

Helen: "I don't blame you, Claire; you've done your share. It's best for all
of us to put Ma into a nursing home while she's still capable of adjusting.
No need for anyone to be upset."

She gives us permission.

The kids are in an uproar. Lori phones Jon and Karen; they both call me
back to bawl me out. "Are you kicking Grandma out?"

How can I answer them? Do they know how their father and I wait for
her to call out during the night? Have they forgotten their own irritation
with her going through their drawers, her letting the bathroom water
flood over the sink when we're in a drought? Can't they understand how
confined I've felt this last year?

Yes, Bad Guy Mom is kicking Grandma out, putting her on an ice floe the
way Eskimos used to do with their elderly when they could no longer
survive on their own.

May 5

Maury is looking into nursing homes. He can't find exactly what he
wants. Meanwhile he's been cleaning out Ma's closets. Didn't realize how
much I'd let them go; what a total mess. I'll be patient, I will.

Ma's not looking well these days. Frail, silent.

May 11

Ma complains that she's dizzy and can't see; yet when Maury comes in, she spots him immediately. And I've watched her browsing the papers.

"Are you still dizzy?" I ask her.

"I'm better. My son is here now."

May 17

Anna informs us that she can only work for us another two weeks. She's pregnant. It doesn't matter now anyway.

May 24

We've made a decision. Ma will go to the Muir Manor Nursing Home on June 15. It's one of the most difficult decisions we've ever made in our lives. The other places we looked at were either far away, had bad reputations, long waiting lists, or exorbitant "entrance fees" where you buy your way in.

Maury doesn't think the Manor is a better place because it's privately owned; he just couldn't bring himself to put Ma's savings in his account so she'd qualify for a state agency. Now every penny she saved will go to the Manor for monthly payments. If she lives more than two years, Maury's family will have to start paying.

And I sit here and write—my heart is broken.

1:00 A.M., In Bed

Am I dreaming or awake? Against her will, Claire has become the matriarch. Claire is the one who makes the decisions. She sees the whole, the passing years, the once strong Hilda fading farther and farther into the distance. Claire with her four children, one husband, one mother-in-law, and two parents must live out her life more freely, spaciously. She can only give so much. Hold fast, Claire, hold fast.

June 16, 1988

Maury packed her bags and left with her early yesterday morning. Grateful the girls weren't around. Only once she was in the car did he tell her where she was going. He narrates the event in a monotone.

"She didn't say a word; she only asked if I believed in an afterlife."

"How did you answer?"

"I said the way we remember the person—that's the afterlife. Can I bring her home one weekend?"

I swallow hard and remain silent. As if Witch Claire might say no.

I've a whole new world of nursing homes to learn about.

June 17

Arnold called about Ma's money last night. Don't even want to know what he said.

Is what we've done irreversible? Too numb to feel anything.

June 19

I've gone through Ma's room and cleaned out the clothes she no longer wears, ancient rent receipts she brought from Saint Louis, letters from people long dead, old jewelry, nightgowns, torn bras.

The quiet is healing. Maury and I went for a long walk. In some ways I know he was waiting for me to make this decision because he couldn't do it himself.

June 20

We go to a film; he calls Rodin a bastard for doing what he wants. I fume at Camille for allowing herself to go mad. Pretty soon we're ranting at each other. Good thing this is merely a film, and we walk home blindly holding hands.

Yes, something else is going on here, still a lot of anger between us.

June 21

Visited the Manor with Maury for the first time. I dreaded confronting her. She kept asking, "Am I in the hospital? When can I come home?"

Hard to know how to answer. For a moment she wouldn't look at me. When she finally said, "It's nice to see you, Claire," I fogged up and let Maury do the talking.

"You'll stay here for now, Ma. There are good nurses to take care of you. Anna's pregnant and can't come to the house anymore."

"I can stay home without Anna. I can get into the tub by myself."

Her roommate, twenty years younger, dumped there for months by relatives while she "convalesces from a broken leg," has been both bossy and protective, as if Ma could care. All Ma wants to know is when she's coming home.

June 22

My first visit alone. The place is small and clean; the help keep it "cheerful" with activities, "picnics" on the small outdoor porch decorated for spring—but the sight and smell of the food make me ill.

The people vary. Some seem so bright I wonder what they're doing there. Others are in bad shape. One woman, no more than seventy, has a degenerative brain disease and has lost her ability to speak. Ma eats her meals, ignoring their blank faces. She was always so proud, felt herself more intelligent than other elderly people she met.

Now that the kids are finished blaming me, they blame their aunt, and in an odd way, I defend Helen. Amy says, "I feel bad Grandma had to go, but lately our house was getting so depressing that Dad didn't even know he was down."

So far none of them wants to visit.

June 23

I've heard you ask if Claire's the one who says you can't come home anymore. Yes, she put you in that place because Helen and Arnold wouldn't share in your care. I've heard you cry and ask why must you stay among strangers when you have three good children. You never could face the fact that your children aren't as good as you like to think.

June 24

Ma has got her days and nights confused. Until she "becomes adjusted" (whatever that means—I already hate the idea), they're giving her tranquilizers. Maury's had a fit.

Tears came today. Turning in final grades, I met an instructor who said I looked "worn and tired." Began to pour out my feelings. If we had talked any longer, I'd have gone home with him!

July 1

Another summer. More stable now, especially if I don't visit too much. I stay home and spend all morning in front of Jon's old computer writing stories about the elderly. My shoulders ache. I've created a grouchy middle-aged character who seems a lot like me!

July 3

I feel for those aides. They work so hard and get so little pay. Garbage collectors make three times more than they do. We're a country with our priorities screwed up.

July 7

Maury put up a calendar where we mark our names on the days we visit so she feels less alone. Wish some of our friends would come, but so far, not one of them has offered; it's hard to ask them.

July 12

Maury's birthday, but we don't feel like celebrating. Just a small cake at home.

July 15

A terrible moaning from one of the rooms. If I just stop by and touch the woman, will I break the cycle? I walk through the halls; people call out: "Do you want to buy my car?" "Lady, can you get me out of here?" I ignore them, make my way to Ma's room, saving my energy for her.

Her roommate has been transferred, she has a new one who never even looks at her. How is it possible that two women can lie so close to one another, yet barely see each other, not communicate at all?

On my way out, that piercing sound again. Will I carry it out with me into the summer sun? No. Amazing the way human beings can block out suffering and restore ourselves to life.

July 29

Ma has refused to eat for the last three days. If this continues, she'll have to go on intravenous feedings.

August 1

Dream: I'm alone with Ma in my old childhood apartment. She's on a pull-out bed and keeps slipping off. Stick-like legs hang out of her nightgown. She shouts. "I want to sleep in your parents' bed!" Astounded, I try to help. She pushes me away, rummages through my mother's dresses, throws everything around. Then her body transforms itself into one of my young black students, Hattie Gray. Ma is Hattie. I watch the transformation, amazed. We go outside into the black ghetto and Ma/Hattie talks to a small black kid on a go-cart, saying, "Be careful, darling. I want you to go upstairs and eat." We start up. By now I'm not sure if Ma is Hattie or not. The living room fills with people who sit on folding chairs, as if this were shiva, *and we're mourning for the dead. I tell them about the transformation. No one believes me. There's Ma herself in her nightgown, weak again. I scream, "She was Hattie just a minute ago. She was walking around!" People think I'm mad. I begin to think so too.*

August 3

She's decided to eat at last. Thank God she won't have to be tube-fed. She tells us, "You have to be good if you want to be treated good in this place." She's even tried to walk to the bathroom alone, saying, "They are busy here. I must help them."

Maybe she thinks that if she's cooperative, she'll get out of "this hospital." One of the nurses commented, "Boy, we sure don't have many patients like her. She's real nice, a good girl."

I'm infuriated. Sure, she's a "good girl," because she hardly demands anything.

On my way out, Ma smiles weakly, "Better to suffer a little than to lie dead in the grave, darling."

August 5

Notes from *Necessary Losses* by Judith Viorst: It is important to establish a strong personal identity so one doesn't overrelate with another person and suffer his miseries.

August 6

At a weekend seminar on death and dying: Once a mother dies, we can't resolve any of our ambivalent feelings. We must give up the fantasy of the omnipotent, idealized parent.

I don't say much, wondering how I'll ever face my own parents' demise. Someone admits she can't accept her father's death: "I pretend he's still alive, that I just haven't talked to him in a while."

Another woman: "I didn't mourn when my mother died; I mourned for her months before."

A newly arrived Chinese man remains hurt that his Americanized children refuse to visit their aunt's grave. Two younger women try to explain their reaction: "Maybe it's meaningless for your sons to drag up old emotions."

The man protests, "No, no. We must honor the dead, even if she is not the mother."

His expectations are so different from theirs.

August 12

We begin a two-week vacation to Alaska tomorrow. Maury has notified the Manor where we'll be. Have such a hard time leaving; sometimes it's harder for me than for him. Always think she'll die, and we won't make it back for her funeral. Once we're gone, I'll put her out of my mind, but until then, the tyranny of the weak grips me.

August 27

We're back. She didn't die, and for the first time the kids took the responsibility on themselves to visit. We're so grateful! Rested from the trip, I was able to sit with her a long time today. An older man asked me how come "my mother" is "in this place" when she's so alert compared to his wife. According to him, Ma belongs at home with us.

Coping with illness is such a personal thing, one that others can never fairly judge.

September 1

Instead of going to Ma, I chose to visit Celia the other day. Dressed up, she cried that she'd been "expecting" visitors all day. She snapped out of her gloom and decided to "entertain," prove she was still functioning.

She recited German poetry and sang *lieder*. Since I didn't have a chair, I sat at her feet. For a moment I actually envied the old woman for her daring spirit. I became part of her small band of German-Jews who escaped to Israel in the late thirties. She spoke with the passion of a woman who was once able to grasp life, to fathom the meaning of it all. During those forty-five minutes we both inhabited another time and space.

Thank you, Celia, for making me aware of my own narrow views. It wasn't nice of me to wake you in the midst of your reverie and ask you if you needed help to the toilet. For those forty-five minutes, whether you were dry or wet wasn't important to you. And for me it felt better to listen to you than to struggle with Ma's silence.

September 4

Dream: We're in a dark basement, some place from my childhood. It's damp, and a lot of old clothes are lying around. Ma comes in dressed in her thin nightgown. She mumbles in Yiddish how badly I'm treating her.

"You have no respect. You don't say hello or good-bye when you leave the house." I defend myself. She starts to cry and to curse old age, wishing on me what I've done to her.

September 10

Today, for the first time, Maury brought Ma home to visit. He waited until he felt she was firmly established in the Manor so she wouldn't become confused and think we were taking her back. Because the aides are so slow in getting patients out of bed, he left early to get her, dressed her himself, pushed her in the wheelchair, put her into the car, then drove home. I took her to the toilet and gave her lunch.

We hoped the visit might break up the tedium of her routine, but she seemed depressed, cognizant of the fact that we wouldn't keep her and that she'd return to the Manor. She slept all afternoon until Maury took her back at 3:00.

"I can't stay here in my son's house?" she asked, as Maury wheeled her out to the car.

How long will it take before she stops asking, and when will I harden enough to say no without getting upset?

We'll try it again next week.

September 17

Same as last weekend. Maury says it's more unsettling than beneficial. How time-consuming and draining for both of us. Some of the elderly are able to leave the Manor, even go shopping, but with Ma, I don't think the effort is worth the results.

September 24

Maury decides we *must* "get Ma out." We take her on a ferry ride to Sausalito; Amy comes along and helps push Grandma's wheelchair up the ramp. Ma is chilled and seasick, silent the whole trip. When we wheel her off the ferry, she shakes her head, "No more boats for me. One boat from Poland to America is enough."

September 30

Fran tells me Celia is quite ill. No visits today. Instead, I feel like doing something exciting and daring.

October 2

An abrasion on Ma's foot won't heel. Maybe she hurt herself on the wheelchair. She now wears big foamy house shoes even when she lies down, never slips on the expensive handmade shoes Maury ordered last December.

October 7

When I went into Ma's room today, two aides were turning her over. She was so listless, I couldn't think of a thing to say. Remembered the advice of my support group: Accept silence, don't fear it.

She looked me over in my T-shirt, stained and sweaty, my hair looking awful. "Claire darling, you are a beautiful young woman." Choked up, I left.

How tenuous life, how short.

October 24

During my visit, Ma had a cramp. Luckily, I got one of the attendants to toilet her. Two nurses helped with a suppository. It's hard to keep after them; they're always so harried, but if I don't pin them down, God knows what will happen. I need to work on assertiveness—but not get so defensive.

November 3

Maury: "There's been a change in her, Claire. She's doing well. It's that new Chinese woman Nelly who's taking care of her. She spends extra time with her. You've no idea what a difference it makes to have caring people with her. Claire? Where are you going?"

(I walk off in silence.) My cousin Nancy died today. She was forty-six, do you hear? Forty-six and brilliant. Don't tell me about your mother.

November 18

Nelly quit. She had real talent but felt she wasn't being paid enough for it. A shame. Why can't the aides earn more money and get more recognition? No young person with ambition will stay on this job.

November 24, Thanksgiving

An aide dresses Ma in her Sunday best: green dress, green pin, and green earrings from the "common pile." She stares at us through her wrinkles and beams. She *is* better, and now I'm sorry we aren't taking her home for turkey. She's even talkative.

"Such beautiful teeth, Maury darling, from all the milk you drank. Shine them like a kiddush cup. Take care and polish your gift."

We've brought her chicken and potatoes, which she likes. Maury's discovered a nonalcoholic foamy malt drink she guzzles down. She's put on a few pounds from the damn stuff. It tastes terrible.

I tease her. "You like beer, Ma?"

"Beer? Then I am a shikker, a drunk. Take it away."

"It's like beer, but it's not beer; you can drink all you want," we say.

She wouldn't drink another drop, and I'm sorry for my little joke.

November 27

A bout of flu and diarrhea has hit the place. The Manor is empty of visitors. There's one change: the wife of one of the male residents who died takes his place. She used to help at lunchtime in exchange for a free lunch for herself. A few of the ambulatory people are still out for the holiday weekend. So far, Ma's okay, but Maury's as worried as he was when we sent Amy off to kindergarten knowing all the kids had colds.

November 30

Hi, Ma, how are you? Look what bargains I've bought, all these shirts. Aren't they pretty? Would you like me to try them on? Do you want a sweatshirt like this? I'll get one for you. How much? Not much at all. What color? Gold. That will look good on you. Gold. I've got to go now. I just came for a minute. I can't stay, but next time I come, I'll bring you a shirt, okay?

December 9, Sixth Day of Chanukah

Maury brings a menorah and candles for Ma to light. He's jittery about the ulcer on her heel.

"You've got to expect things to go wrong," I scold.

"This is plain stupid."

One of the aides "dolled" her up. She lies there looking angelic with her hair curled childishly about her cheeks. Not agitated like Lillian who wheels into the room and stares at Maury.

He smiles at her. "Hello, Lillian. Happy Chanukah. We all love you."

Her face crumbles. "Huh? What's Chanukah?"

"It's a holiday, anyone can celebrate it. Do you want to join us?"

"Why isn't my family here? Why didn't they come on this Chanukah? They never come. They don't love me."

"Yes, they do, that's why they sent you here where you get good care."

Lillian begins to cry. "God bless you, Mister. That lady over there is lucky to have you for a son."

On the way out, I don't wish Ma happy Chanukah for fear she'll say her prayer: We should all live until 120 and celebrate together again next year, amen.

December 23, Our Anniversary

> *You are gone at midnight to meet our daughter / she waits in town*
> *without a jacket / the warmth of our bed has cooled in your*
> *absence / bedroom screens creak / in the wind / even with the*

weight of two nightgowns / I lie here chilled / mumbling in my
mind / I want to tell you / how I see my life clearing / how I'm
learning to sit in the silence / the ease of my bones curling into you
the last twenty-two years / like the only pair of matched socks / in
the laundry

December 27

She continues to hold her head high, refuses to cry out about her indignities, unlike the others. During our visit, Maury was upset that her stockings and panties were placed in the "community drawer," and the aide put her in adult diapers.

"This isn't a charity ward. We pay for better care." He insists, "She doesn't need diapers; they can use underpants if they watch her and toilet her every two hours."

Amazing that she does stay dry most of the time.

A new woman wears the Serenities her daughter brings; she doesn't like the roughness of the Manor's diapers. Still, her daughter says the Manor's the best nursing home in the neighborhood; they've tried six different ones.

Meanwhile, Maury complains about the level of "inefficiency" and how the place is overpriced.

December 30

She's been agitated all day, thinks someone is stealing from her. Her blue sweater was misplaced for three days; it turned up in Lillian's drawer—I'm sure by accident, but Ma grumbled about the incident. How aware she is at times.

December 31

Stopped in for five minutes today on my way to Berkeley. An old woman was on the pot.

"Damn it to hell, get me off this shit toilet."

An aide reprimanded her. "Now, no more four-letter words. I'll be there as soon as I can. I've four other people to check."

"I don't care. How about 'blab, blab, poop, poop,' does that make you happy? Just get me outta this shit hole!"

1989

The second stage of beauty is eternal

January 1, 1989, New Year's Day

A new year, what's new in my heart?

That not everything about aging is bad. To be oneself at last. Free of the opinions of others. To live as one wants. A centeredness, an inner direction. A lessening of both disappointment and expectation. To watch a rerun of a Charles Laughton film, terrifying in childhood, and to laugh at it. To feel free of the fear of sex, to enjoy small pleasures that went unnoticed before, a cloudy day when I can stay inside and rest, without being driven to "do something." To accept that there is a natural end to all things.

January 3

I watch a cheerful white-haired woman feed her speechless husband. He mechanically opens his mouth and sucks down the mush. She buzzes about, pleasantly humming and stuffing him with special treats, wiping his lips with a napkin. Would that I grow old like that.

The cheerful woman walks over to Ma and me. "Hello there, you nice people."

Ma hesitates a moment, then says, "Please meet my son's wife, she's not a nobody. She is a teacher."

I blush. If Ma harbors anger at me, she doesn't show it.

January 4

My mother is ill suddenly. I'll have to fly back East soon. How long will it be before I'm in Maury's shoes?

January 5

Started a book on Sufi beliefs about death. The theme: No need to suffer if you believe in reincarnation and the restoration of the spirit.

January 10

Today is Mrs. Witt's birthday. She must be in her late nineties. She's parked in the hallway line-up of wheelchairs that have no place to go.

"I want my pencil! I want my pencil!" she shouts. The male aide won't give it to her. She might hurt herself, and, legally, he'd be at fault. He's an alcoholic, but the director keeps him on, desperate for male care. Everyone's so worried about lawsuits they forget to be human.

For a moment we step out from Ma's room. Maury knows Sarah Witt from frequent visits and gives her a pencil. She shakily scratches out S-A-R. Just then her son, who looks about seventy-five, walks in; immediately he becomes upset with his mother's writing. We stare at him as he begins to grill her:

"Mother, is it true you wet your pants? Do you know who is president? Do you know who George Washington is?"

Embarrassed, we pretend we aren't watching and turn toward Ma, who's also in her wheelchair but in her room. Mr. Witt peeks in. Now it's his chance to stare at us as Maury lifts Ma to her bed.

"A jumping kangaroo from Australia," Maury quips, pretending she's lifting herself. Mr. Witt's eyes widen.

Ma smiles weakly and plays the game. "A kangaroo from Saint Louis, not from Australia."

Witt looks stunned.

"Pardon me, Mrs. Brenner, is it? Would you mind telling me how you get your mother to be so responsive?"

"She's my husband's mother, not mine. Ask him, he'll give you all the tips you need."

January 12

I wait the last minute to tell her: "I've got to fly back East, Ma. My mother's having surgery."

"Oh, I am sorry. A safe journey, Claire. I am sad for your parents that they don't have you with them all the time the way I do."

And I'm off.

February 5

Flew in yesterday morning. My mind still humming with the tales of the young woman forest ranger from Alaska who sat next to me on the return flight. I've become so bogged down with family issues, I've forgotten what a big world is out there! Time to be like Lori: "Not me, I'll never get old."

My mother is recovering from her bladder suspension. She isn't doing badly, but I have a suspicion it's not going to work. She needs an exacting routine for security. Dad, on the other hand, is willing to try things, even though his world, too, has become constricted by health and age.

How the old neighborhood has changed; every time I visit, the streets bustle with new immigrants—Koreans, Greeks, and Russians. But inside the Hirsch domicile, everything remains the same: the white sofa under yellowed plastic seat covers that squeak when you sit on them, Mom's breakfront a masterpiece of the fifties with its porcelain figures and teacups. Dad's car groans in his shack of a garage. I still get a kick out of driving it. I remember the woman in my support group last year who gave everything of her father's away within three weeks of his death. Not me (Lori again), can't imagine ever giving Dad's Dodge Dart away.

In my old environment, something happens that makes me fall back into childhood roles, yet I need to be the adult if I'm going to take care of my old parents—something to work on and prepare myself for in the near future.

February 7

Ma must have sensed my absence because she asked me today if Maury and I were still married. Spouses you can divorce, but not parents. I experienced that with my own parents these past weeks. Now that I'm home, I keep rerunning the tapes I played with both of them in my head.

February 15

Phoned Arnold last week, and bawled him out for his lack of support. Thought it was a useless gesture, but for the first time in months a letter from him addressed to Ma and Maury arrived today. Was ready to champion my victory over Maury in "family management," until Maury read his P.S.: "Whatever you do, don't let Ma die."

Thanks Arnold, especially since you're not here to help. Too bad you weren't with me yesterday when I arrived at the Manor, and Ma was digging out her bowels with her fingernails because the aides couldn't get to her fast enough.

February 20

No, Claire didn't make the Jell-O; no, the nurse in the hallway isn't the cleaning lady. No, Claire doesn't want to eat lunch here. I tell Maury about my visit; he defends her, "Anyone would become forgetful living in that environment."

Tried to talk him into a weekend away in March. He offhandedly said something about Helen coming "to cover" while we're gone. "She'd come if you wouldn't intimidate her."

"How am I so 'intimidating'?"

"You don't see yourself the way others do. Sometimes you don't know your own strength."

February 24

Maybe he's right about his sister. I *can* be a bitch. Maybe I should feel bad for her. All that misplaced anger.

February 27

Is it my imagination or were people at the party last night cool to Maury? "Well, is he coming or does he have to stay and feed Mommy again?" they asked snidely. Why did I even mention his feeding her to everyone? A perverse pride on my part that makes others guilt-ridden. Despite all my protestations, I felt sensitized to his being the butt of a joke.

March 14

The beautiful old bodies at the local pool, one as old as Ma, wrinkled, bent, but swimming still. Let them be my guides, my mentors. Let me think of them, their independence, and not become fixated on every new wrinkle or pain, or whether I'll have enough money to survive old age.

March 18

An article in the *New Republic* on "greedy geezers" who care nothing about youth: they desire only to live in luxurious retirement communities, apart from the rest of the world. No longer useful to their culture or the next generation, a generation which may rise up and rebel against them.

True, some people are like this, but should the rest of us suffer for the rich? Sounds like a distorted way of thinking about the aged. Claude Pepper's proposal that the Feds pay for part of nursing care costs never even got off the floor.

March 24

Dream: My day off. Maury's planned an outing on which I must take Ma. We're with other seniors on a bus driving to a health spa. Ma sits in a wheelchair, her head nodding. We arrive; the place is cultish, heavily supervised, everyone obeys orders exactly. Four spiral staircases lead down to pools of water. I have trouble maneuvering Ma's wheelchair.

She asks me to take her to the farthest level. I struggle with the chair but can't make it. We miss lunch. Now the staff won't feed her. I'm livid, screaming, "You can't do this; give her anything, an apple, an egg. I'll report you at once."

Still they refuse. "Give her some food! She has low blood sugar; she'll die if she doesn't eat! Then you'll have a court case on your hands!"

The mummified staff walks into the kitchen. Meanwhile, Ma insists on going down to yet another pool no one knows about. I manage to wheel her to a child's wading pool where a few old people bathe. She stands up, gets out of her chair, then crawls on her hands and knees into the water. I watch her with amazement; I don't stop her. She's wearing my old black bathing suit. I'm happy she has a moment of pleasure. She bobs up and down. Then suddenly I don't see her. I'm frightened, wonder if I should jump in. Do it, I tell myself, you'll look like you caused her death. There'll be an investigation. I jump in; it's too late. I carry out her limp body in my arms.

April 3

March has come and gone and we didn't get away, but we did drive to the city on Sunday. Stopped at the Manor on the way home. I forget the contrast between the vitality of San Francisco and this place—its elderly shrieking, passing gas, and always, the smell of institutional food.

Emptied of her last vestige of strength and sex, Ma sat on the bed in her "undershirt" (she no longer wears bras) unwilling to eat.

Maury dragged her like a white limp doll onto the toilet. "Don't waste so much paper, darling. I don't need it."

I want to throw a bomb, blow everyone up, stop this absurd system.

April 20, Passover

We bring Ma home; three months since her last visit here. Some of our guests are patient with her; others, probably with hang-ups about their own parents, avoid her. She looks stunned, as if to say, "So, this is the real world."

After the second cup of wine, she asks to lie down. At 9:00 P.M. Maury excuses himself, and drives her back to the Manor. I entertain our guests alone, steer the conversation away from "Maury and his mother."

When everyone's left, he returns, exhausted. The same question. Was it worth it? If only we knew what she was thinking.

April 23

That her basic goodness and sweetness remain is remarkable.

"Come in, Maury. I could have made a nice lunch for you and your wife. How pretty you look, Claire, like a girl. Your body should not know any pain. Karen has a boyfriend? This is his picture? Is he one of ours? He is not large, but with her, his luck should be large. They will have a wedding?"

"He's only a boyfriend," I say.

"A boyfriend today, a husband tomorrow. I have a dress to wear? Bring me my good shoes, too."

Ma's excited, and pleased with her, I capitalize on her liveliness. "When the time's right, I'll take you for a new dress."

Maury whispers, "Take it easy. She's so agitated she nearly rolled out of bed."

To the end the archetypal Jewish Mamma—what is life for a woman without a man?

April 28

Celia died this morning. I didn't know my December visit would be the last. A whole era passes with her. A woman totally different from Ma, a woman who rebelled against her confinement until the end.

To celebrate Celia's life, I went into the health food store and bought myself a tofu sandwich and a sparkling water. Celia would have liked that. The finality is hard to fathom. That striking last shot of Milan Kundera's *The Unbearable Lightness of Being* haunts me: the trees, the joy, the sun, the accident, then the camera stops. There is nothing but darkness.

April 29

We went to Celia's funeral today. Fran asked me if I'd like to say a few words as part of the eulogy. Found myself talking about Celia's positive traits, of seeing her whole and energetic.

Later Fran thanked me. "You know, Mom may have been nurturing to others, but she was a very difficult parent."

How contradictory the roles of parenthood and personhood. Celia nurtured part of my spirit that neither Ma nor my own mother does, but was hard on her own daughter.

The rabbi summed up her life quickly, his words fitting and not embellished. I wondered what he might say of Ma, how the *shiva* will go, but we don't talk about *shiva*. We're too repressed in this family to face it.

May 14, Mother's Day

I return the silk nightgown I bought for Ma. Maury said she needs something more practical for the nursing home. I bring her a cotton one.

"Maury didn't think you'd use the silk one."

"I wear it, not Maury. I like silk." Then she adds, "Wait. Don't tell him, don't make him feel bad."

This from a woman who can't remember from one day to the next, whose vision is dimming so that she thinks any male approaching in the hallway is her son.

June 2

> *She is ill / death does not take her / she will not eat / death does not take her / others die / others are missing each week / death does not take her / she loses bodily flesh each day / death does not come*

June 3

She barely speaks. She's down to 105 pounds. Part of Maury dies. He spends half an hour feeding her lunch, then calls Helen and arranges for her to fly out to see her mother "for the last time." Finally, he asks the kids to visit. They all hedge with their responses. Please Ma, don't die on the day of Lori's graduation.

June 9

Cancel it. Call everyone back. She's better again. Forget the visits, kids. We can have Lori's party after all. Don't worry, your grandma lives forever.

June 15, Ma's One-Year Anniversary in the Manor

Maury brought Ma home, while I escaped from their "routine" and the overriding sense of death. He has more need for her to eat than she does herself.

Where did I escape to? To a friend's, and what did we talk about? Her mother's savings drying up from payments to a convalescent home, her brother's lack of involvement. A predictable American family pattern by now.

July 1

Ma's roommate died this week. I didn't even know. Wonder if Ma does. The nurse says she picked at her scalp all week. The two of them always ignored one another. Still, she must sense the empty bed next to hers.

July 3

Maury's been irritable all weekend. Tonight he admitted, "It's the damn situation, that's what it is."

"You don't *have* to go every day. Would it really matter so much if you went every other day? You'll wear yourself out and make me a young widow."

He explodes. "Until she doesn't know the difference, I'll handle Ma the best way I know how. Don't tell me what to do with my mother. I don't tell you how to handle your parents. You know that volunteer, Paula? She comes just as much as I do, and she's an adopted daughter."

"Are you trying to tell me that I should go every day too?"

"I didn't say that. I just said there are people who are capable of daily visits."

"Let's stop this conversation. Look, can't you be more emotionally balanced about this, more objective? You're upsetting yourself."

"Emotionally balanced—when my mother's dying?"

"She's been 'dying' for a long time now."

"You can be a bitch, can't you? First you want her out. Now you don't want me to visit her so much."

I leave the room and slam the bedroom door shut.

July 8

Today I stayed for two hours. When I arrived, Ma was on the toilet shouting her head off. I forgot how she could swear.

"Goddamn it, get me off here. My tuches hurts. Doesn't anyone hear me, you louses?"

Who knows how long she'd been sitting there? I sidetracked a young aide who awkwardly laughed, called another aide, and together the two of them put Ma back in bed and sponged her down, no easy task despite her small size.

It's a long time since I've seen Ma's body; her limbs are bone-thin. Her wrists and ankles look like they could crack. Her once beautiful breasts hang flat against her stomach. Strange, in a way it was a relief to see her—after I myself try so hard to conform to the mannequin perfection of magazines. Yes, this is how women look when they get old, no matter whether they're Marilyn Monroe or Hilda Brenner—or Claire Brenner. The sooner I become accustomed to a body that's not ageless, the better off I'll be.

Despite Ma's bedsores, she quieted down and looked calm in a cotton dress that Helen had sent her.

"I hurt. I didn't like sitting there so long. No one helped me," she said apologetically.

July 9

Went to the drugstore and picked up some calcium tablets and vitamins. Think I've lost a quarter of an inch in height.

July 11

Ma's doing better. She puts her hands on her breasts. "There's no milk here for my children."

"Your children are grown, Ma."

"Even if children are big, they need a mother. They always need a mother."

I look away, and run across the street to buy her a yogurt, but I just can't go back to the Manor. End up pacing the mall and eating the yogurt myself.

July 19

Today I made up my mind. I *did* manage to get there. An obese aide was trying to get Ma to drink. I myself was intimidated by her. I thought Ma would be too, that maybe she felt Suzette was trying to "hurt her," but when I watched the two of them together, I was amazed and touched.

Inside that huge body came out the sweet voice of a child. "Who's been kissin' and huggin' Grandma today?"

"You," Ma grinned from ear to ear.

And that beautiful, big, strong black arm held my crumbling mother-in-law's face in her hand.

July 20

We're leaving for a week's vacation. Tensions are running high. We stop to see Ma. Maury lingers at her bed while I give him that "you're too involved" look. He retorts before I speak.

"I *am* making an effort. When we come back I'll rearrange her room and make it into a study for you. The room's yours."

I'm shocked. We've kept her room empty and untouched for over a year. This is a big step for Maury.

July 27

Good-bye Tahoe. Good-bye lake and trees and silent heart. We're going back to Grandma. We don't go too far or stay too long lest she die. She's waiting for us with her stale breath and open arms. "My children, my children, thank God you returned."

August 1

Silently she sits, greets me without moving a muscle in her face. I tell her we've been away. She will not look at me, will not eat, but when an aide takes her tray, she shouts, "Give me my food. Give me back my food." Then, "Can I come home now? I'm not so dizzy." She moves her hand about aimlessly; it jumps like a grasshopper.

I become old and dizzy myself. I become like my teenage neighbor scorning his mother, "You've ruined my day."

August 9

The dead heat of summer. Even so, the days pass quickly with a sense of the transience of all life, her spirit an apparition following me everywhere. At the allergist's, I read *People Magazine*: a mother cries she didn't think her son would put her away; a son cries he has no words.

I have done this, not the son.

August 10

Dreams of death and failure. An old professor challenges me to teach a course I can't manage. Ma, white as a ghost, is carried out on a stretcher to a nursing home. I'm writing long, beautiful letters to Helen.

She sits at the dining table staring into space, thrusting her tongue out. Everyone else is eating. I wheel her into her room and try to feed her. Two bodies creep after me to see what's going on—one, a confused woman unable to speak, and the other, a rare old man. I tell myself, Reach out, offer them the cookies you've brought.

"Would you like one?" I ask hesitantly, offering the tray.

"Get away from me—you're trying to poison me," the man screams and wheels out. The woman follows.

Ma begins to eat. She blesses every bite of food, then repeatedly spits it out.

I restrain my anger.

"Why are you spitting everything out?"

"I am tired of eating. The glass is too heavy. I cannot hold it."

As I lift the juice to her lips, she studies me. "Am I wasting?"

"Yes, you're wasting."

"It is not good to waste God's food. We must be thankful to Him. He gives us health. He takes care of us."

"Good, how about some jam on your pancake?"

She spits it out. I try a lighter tone. "You're a fussy eater."

"I am not fussy. Every person likes to enjoy what they eat."

So something's still working here. Maury says she even played bingo last week with the help of an aide. Didn't believe him, as he always makes everything better than it is, but who knows?

She looks around. "Some people have to read their Bible to say prayers; I don't need one. I know my prayers by heart."

August 20

Lori left for San Francisco State this morning. I cried more with her going than with Jon and Karen. In the last few years my life has changed drastically. Somehow I need her around, her outgoingness, her inventiveness. She infused me with youth.

August 31

Lori home from San Francisco for a few hours to pick up some things. She decided to visit Grandma on her own.

"Grandma was strange. She wanted me to climb into bed with her because I was 'tired.' Maybe she thinks I'm still a little kid. She asked if we could bake cookies, you know, those hard butter bullets loaded with sugar and fat, the ones she used to make and I'd sneak. Then she really said something weird. She asked me not to leave her because two 'bums' might come in off the street and 'take her away in a van.' "

Say not a word. Be happy Lori visited, happy that Ma had some reactions, emotions. Better than nothing. Don't suggest to your kids that if they visited more often, maybe Grandma wouldn't become so confused when she sees one of them. But please, one thing: don't tell her we now have extra room here.

September 9

I've started teaching a new composition class. I explain Plato's idea of beauty to a group of eighteen-year-olds:

> *The second stage of beauty surpasses the first of physical beauty; it is more valuable than the beauty of the body. It is eternal; it*

neither comes into being nor passes away; it is not anything
corporeal; it is absolute, existing alone with itself in such a manner
that it neither undergoes any increase nor suffers any changes.

I look up and hear myself say, "Here's an example. When I look at my mother-in-law now compared to a picture of her at sixteen, all her external beauty has faded, but a greater beauty has replaced it."

I'm amazed at my own words.

After class, a long-haired boy comes up to me and says, "You know, my grandma lived with us until she was ninety-one. My mom took care of her. Even though Gram was hunchbacked, her spirit dwarfed some of the tallest people I've ever met."

September 13

Amy comes with us to see Grandma; Lori meets us at the Manor. Lately she seems intent on seeing Grandma.

An elderly musician, ringed by a circle of wheelchairs, plays a cello for them. Ma sits lamenting, "I'm dizzy, I'm dizzy."

The cellist decides to play a few Hebrew melodies. A few old people not familiar with the words hum along anyway. I can't contain the tears. Lori's furious, nudges me in the ribs, "Cut it out, Mom; stop feeling sorry for yourself."

I ask Amy, "Which one will I look like when I'm old?"

She doesn't respond to my display of weakness. Both girls are taken with a new woman who is wheeled in. Her beautiful long white hair, rare in this place, catches their eyes.

Ma smiles at us and asks Maury, "Are you my father or Arnold? Can I please go to my home now?"

September 20

Gave Ma the watermelon I'd brought. At first she refused it, but once she started to eat, she couldn't stop. She kept putting her hand into the bowl and taking chunks of it out. I was getting worried when suddenly she stopped flat and looked across the room.

"See that woman over there? She eats too much, and her bosom is too big. Only young women need such bosoms."

I nearly laughed out loud.

September 22

Ma's very ill. She was taken to the hospital for dehydration. She refuses to eat or drink. Maury came home exhausted.

"If I had the guts, I swear I'd slip her a few Nembutal and let it be over," he muttered.

Does he want me to encourage him, tell him that I dreamt I hired some-one to finally end this? Why can't he? Why can't the doctor on call?

Midnight

If there were some legislation in favor of euthanasia, that too could prove a dangerous and misused thing unless there were many safeguards.

September 23

In the hospital, watching her sleep, I thought she'd passed over to the other side. When she woke, I offered her a bit of food; she accepted. Secretly I hoped she wouldn't, that death would come, quietly, easily.

September 24

Maury: "Another day like this, and she'll be comatose."

I stay away. Last time I visited, she was frightened, called me her "friend," wouldn't let go of my hand. She's down to a hundred pounds. How terrible to die alone away from family.

September 25

Spent the morning on the phone calling the kids, told them this might be the end. Maury and I've been quarreling over whether they should fly back to Saint Louis for the funeral. I say yes—no matter the cost or what they're doing. He says let them honor their grandmother while she's still alive; let them visit her now.

He warns, "Don't go if you're going to start one of your 'fits.'"

Don't worry. I'll manage to smile. I've had good training. After the funeral, I'll pretend everything's been just fine between your family and me all these months.

September 26

At last he vents some rage: "Let her die, damn it. I can't do anything more. Let her be buried in the ground next to Pa."

Glad he expressed himself; it eases my own guilt and that which is nearly impossible for him.

September 28

Maury called Helen. She *may* fly out. I don't have to internalize her problems as my own and take on her responsibility. And what about my responsibility to my own mother? How will I behave if she becomes ill?

September 29

Scapegoats. Have I used Ma as one? I call Fran and ramble on about my life.

"She's been in the Manor fifteen months, and what have I accomplished that I couldn't have done with her here?"

"Claire Brenner, are you nuts? Why do you always have to test yourself, question everything you do? You *deserve* to have peace and quiet in your home."

October 1

The crisis has passed. She's recovering, but Helen is coming anyway.

October 3

Ma was stable enough to leave the hospital and return to the Manor. Now she's a "feeder," down to pureed foods, hand spooned in a "special" room. A group of six women who refuse to eat by themselves sit around a small table and are fed by aides. The thought of it is as upsetting as the food itself, but she's gained back a few pounds.

Maury and I visited together. "Eat, Ma, or you'll die. Do you want to die?" he shouted.

Slowly she sucked in the awful mush. She weighs ninety-nine pounds.

As I started to pace the hall, I bumped into the director, Mrs. Tam. "Don't worry, Mrs. Brenner, she's not dying so fast. She'll live a long time. As long as she eats just enough to keep her alive."

I swear I'm going to stop waiting for her death and live my life.

October 4

Helen arrived yesterday. I cooked for her and Maury, then left the house. A pretty rude gesture, but felt it would be better to leave in order to control my anger. Just couldn't face her. I thought she'd understand, but according to Maury, she was furious. Tonight I, who rant and rave like a child, ended up serving her dinner while she brings me house gifts. What other choice do we have? Whether it's phony or not, this is the way rational adults behave in the world. Maybe if we act this way, we can eventually *feel* better about each other. She's staying at a motel.

Like Maury, she tries to find the bright spots, underplays Ma's illness, won't say Ma is failing. She visits her for such long periods of time, I'm surprised and wonder how she manages.

I call Karen at school to tell her; in her wisdom she says, "I used to think Aunt Helen was a witch the way you talked, but now I see she's petrified of her mother's death. She's trying to protect herself, knowing she's next. Anyone can understand that."

October 13

Yep, it's visiting time again. How about doing something nice for someone else? Okay, Ma, I'll help you with your food, read to you. It will make *me* feel better about myself.

Finally, she speaks: "Please stop, Claire. That reading gives me a big headache."

October 24

A week since the earthquake. Even though we know we're sitting on a tinderbox, who would believe it? We're lucky not to have serious damage out here, but in San Francisco parts of the Bay Bridge collapsed and buildings caught on fire. How the human mind is capable of blocking out potential disaster. How small it is.

October 29

Amy visits Ma this week with her friend Peter and me. He's shy with "Grandmother," maybe thinks she ignores him because he isn't "one of the clan." More likely she can't focus on someone young and new to her. A poignant contrast between their impetuous energy and Ma's lethargy.

At first she calls me "nurse," but when she recognizes me, she says, "Claire darling, I love you. Go into the kitchen and take something to eat. You need to have your strength. Take, Claire darling. Take all the food you want."

I harden myself so I don't go to pieces in front of Amy. Later we talk about our feelings. Want to make this "lesson time" but let it go. While she seems to care, she insists, "Grandma's not alive anymore."

Part of me agrees with my offspring; another part says Ma still has her soul, and that is what keeps her from dying.

November 8

My first visit in two weeks. "She's much better; she's gained four pounds," Maury declares, full of himself. "You don't know how happy I am, Claire."

November 9

The Berlin wall came down today, exactly fifty-one years after *Kristallnacht.* Remember visiting Berlin, a college student, just as the wall went up—ages ago in human time, a drop in space in galactic time. Wonder what it will mean for this generation, the problems it may solve and the problems it will create. I'm learning there are always both consequences to everything.

Such major changes in the world; even if one doesn't feel them right away, they have long-range impact, a reminder that mothers-in-law come and go with illness and eventual death. Why think my case is "special"? Why does my ego dictate a magnified importance about my situation?

November 16

"Look what pretty legs you have, not pudgy, like my family's," I say.

She smiles, then looks around, and for the first time in a long while, asks, "Am I still in the hospital?"

Maury gently reminds her, "You're in the Manor, Ma; they take better care of you here than we could."

Such pain in his voice.

November 18

She remembers little of the recent past (but events years ago); Maury's begun to use the term *Alzheimer's.*

"It has its benefits," he says. "Every day I repeat exactly the same news about the kids, but she doesn't remember. She doesn't remember if she's been in pain or not. It's a blessing."

November 23, Thanksgiving

Maury is determined to get some food into her. We bring along a jar of herring. He gets her out of bed, hands her the herring, and while Ma's roommate gobbles down turkey, Ma picks her herring to pieces. She tells us, "This smells good," and nibbles at the halvah and matzos we've brought. We don't stay long. Maury has promised we'll take a walk together. She looks up and says, "Thanksgiving. All of us together next year too, until a hundred and twenty."

December 12

An elderly hunchbacked aide is having trouble turning Ma over. Orletta can't get a job anywhere else, and this pays a lousy five dollars an hour, even if it breaks her back. Feel more compassion for her than I do for Ma.

Slowly my visits decline. What I once considered so important for both of us doesn't matter much now.

December 16

The anniversary's of Pa's death. How ironic: Ma, who has such poor sense of time and is unaware of the date, asks about him.

"And where is Pa?"

"He died, Ma."

She looks away as if she knows after all, then asks, "How old is Helen?"

"Helen will be sixty."

"My Helen, sixty? How old am I?"

We tell her.

She closes her eyes and doesn't speak anymore.

December 27

Story Idea: The plane spoke a terrible roar from her distant childhood. How such a monster didn't fall out of the sky killing every one, God alone knew. He would have to make the miracle; He would have to guide the way. Her lips mumbled some long-forgotten prayer, whose meaning she didn't understand.

Was her dead husband Moishe floating out there in the blue? Moishe with his foolish schemes to get rich. Let men be for young women. She'd never marry again, like a foolish widow hungry for a pair of pants. Share her bed with some old cocker, wash his clothes, give him her hard-earned money. She'd live alone, bear the loneliness, read, cook, go to her meetings. She wasn't like her lady friends who ran off to Florida every winter. She sat at the edge of her seat, her glasses smashed into her nose, and dreamed.

Manhattan became a toy her great-grandson Michael had built. Damp-eyed, she stared into a clear blue sky, a vastness like after you're dead and rotting in the earth and your soul flies around crying in that blue.

1990

She refuses to speak

January 2, 1990

1990! Already I've written the date twice. Only ten years to the end of the century. Can remember the awe in writing 1950 and 1960, and especially 1984.

Is this decade different from others? Despite all the changes in science and technology, human beings and their emotions remain the same.

Is the significance of dates becoming less or more important as I get older; is my concept of time changing?

But what about concepts of success, achievement? What if I actually get what I want? How long before the excitement wears off and I'll want something else?

And happiness? What is that? A quiet moment when I accept life and who I am.

January 6

Last night on my way home from Berkeley, my car automatically turned at the Manor. I've never visited at night before. It was dark; many of the residents are asleep by seven. For a moment, no one was mumbling or crying out. The quiet brought a kind of comfort.

It was 8:30 P.M. Ma peered out of her room. She still had on her head-phones that Maury brought her for listening to tapes, but nothing was playing. This time she recognized me immediately.

"Claire darling. It's you? I'm starving. Get me some potatoes."

I was shocked; her not eating is such a problem. The Chinese cook, who was washing up, didn't understand I wanted real food; instead he handed me two sickeningly sweet vanilla puddings.

She gobbled one down. Her hand reached into the empty air, as if she were clawing for something but didn't know what. Then she jerked my sleeve saying she wanted more, but when I offered the other pudding, she pushed it away. Wasn't sure she knew who I was any longer. Fed her with a sense of anonymity.

These are the worst years of her long and giving life. Surely her old self wouldn't want this.

January 8

Karen's here for her winter break. We went to visit Grandma. Awed by the sight of Ma, she frowned. "Grandma's more curled up than last year. It's from staying in bed all the time. I guess you can't do much now. Don't feel bad, Mom. If a person lives the first fifty years of life helping others, she can live the rest helping herself."

January 12

Sarah Witt died today. She had just turned ninety-seven, a spirited old lady. Wonder if that's what kept her going so long. Guess we won't see her son anymore or have to compare ways we handle our old parents.

January 21

Apparently friends have been coming to visit, and I knew nothing about it. Today I found a honey cake and a note to Ma on her tray, and last week, some lilacs. I'm so grateful; I wonder if she's aware of her visitors.

February 5

This past weekend when we drove north, Maury didn't even phone the Manor to give them the number of our bed and breakfast.

After our return visit, he told me, "She's become an institutional personality. Better if I don't visit every day. Maybe my presence upsets her. She doesn't even try to take a few steps anymore."

Pacing the hall, I bumped into Mrs. Tam. She took me aside. "In twenty years of business, I've never seen anyone like Mr. Brenner. Don't get me wrong. He's no saint. At first, I couldn't stand his complaints; he expected perfection. We're only human, Mrs. Brenner. You think it's easy to keep this place going? Still, he's a good man."

Yes, Maury can make a nuisance of himself, but that's why Ma lives, and others die.

February 25

Today I found Ma in "wheelchair row" waiting to be fed. How I detest that. Put her breakfast on a tray and wheeled her outside to show her the flowering winter plants.

"Who am I, Ma?"

"Tell her who you are, don't ask," Maury whispers to my conscience. Why did I do that?

She half looked at me. "A nice lady."

"Claire, Ma."

"Claire?"

"Yes."

She reached for my sweater as if she were a child reaching for a new object, something not tainted with the dullness of this place, then pushed it aside, and wanted my purse. Did it remind her of the days when she had her own purse? She looked sad but didn't cry. Almost wished she had.

March 7

A glorious spring day. Full of energy from a dance workshop I attended, able and willing to visit. I buy a sandwich at the deli and bring it to her to see if she'll eat some real food.

In the hallway, a woman grabs me, waving a letter. "Read this to me," she commands. I do. She starts clutching the doll in her arms and crying. The aide shouts down the hall in a friendly voice, "Oh hi, Mrs. B., don't bother with *her*. I already read the letter to her three times this morning. She can drive you crazy."

On to see Ma. Cheerfully, I wheel her into the sunshine. Not once does she open her eyes. "Ma, don't you want to eat this? You like chicken salad."

"Yeah," she says, spitting out every bite.

Eat half the sandwich myself and waste the other half. Getting a bite of it into her is an accomplishment. After twenty minutes I leave, less cheerful than when I entered.

March 15

Today we celebrated Ma's eighty-fifth birthday—we think. Not sure of the year she was born. Maury had planned it for weeks.

I drove to the Manor at 2:30 P.M. Amy was too busy to come; Lori had to stay on campus—maybe it's better, because Ma was in bad shape. Her head drooped to one side; she wouldn't speak, held her arms tightly around her breasts, as if protecting herself from the outside world. She lay at the side of her bed holding onto the rail. Her legs and arms are so thin now.

Five random residents patiently waited for the Safeway angel food cake and melted lime sherbet. They didn't talk with Ma, nor she with them. I was shocked at the sight of those strangers "invited" to her party just so a few bodies would be there. A quiet party at our house would have cheered her more.

Marianne, the social activities director, put on some dated recordings of the music from *Exodus*. Two "guests" Ma refused to look at tried to make conversation. A few of them picked their teeth or their scalps.

Overcame my aversion, smiled a phony smile and talked to a woman about the times she baked birthday cakes for her kids when they were small. Turns out she's a former Berkeley professor.

She chirped out of her ninety-two-year-old paper-thin face, "This is a party for *all* of us, a real occasion."

Here were these old people confined to wheelchairs enjoying a moment of pleasure and dignity, and here was I repulsed by the whole affair. Haven't I learned anything in all this time, haven't I yet learned that people of any age relish the simplest pleasures?

Marianne was full of smiles. Her high grating voice insisted the residents were having a good time.

The afternoon was ludicrous: reading "Birthday Greetings from Barbara and George Bush" (as if Ma votes Republican!) that Marianne "received from the White House" (really from a handy stack in her desk drawer); the silly yellow paper crown slipping off Ma's head, her eyes locked shut; Maury stuffing her, intoning, "Eat your cake," the sherbet dripping onto her bib and lap.

When the party ended, I spoke with Marianne. "Don't you think it would be better if she—gave in and—went?"

She replied coldly, "She's not asking us to help her die, Mrs. Brenner. She liked the party on her own terms."

Hmm. I doubt it, even if others think so.

This evening Maury and I had a raging argument.

"How could you stand there smiling?"

"What do you want me to do?"

"Why can't you ever face reality?"

April 1

Ma is ill again. She hasn't eaten for three days. Maury took her to the hospital for some tests. Nothing serious, but if he hadn't watched over her constantly, we would have lost her. When he was late the other night, I thought he'd walk in and say her long travail is over. Instead he came in cursing.

"Those damn nurses. They don't want to treat her infection. It's one thing to let her die from a heart attack, but it's another to let her die from poor care."

April 9

Got all the girls to visit her while they were home for various breaks. Impossible to gather them together these days. They're so full of themselves. Unrealistic to think of flying them back to Saint Louis for her funeral.

When Helen called, I repeated what I'd said to Marianne at Ma's birthday party—it would be better if Ma "went." Gently said, but she was furious.

"How'd you like it if I said I hope your mother dies?"

"Helen, it's not the same thing. My mother can still function."

And how much longer before my own mother won't be able to function, and I lose my patience with her?

April 18

Something wonderful has happened! A love affair!

Yes, the new man in his eighties, a retired eye doctor, and the former Berkeley professor! He insists he wants to "lie down to rest" with her in her bed. Some of the staff is pleased; it's the first time I've seen any real life happening in the Manor. Some nurses think it's a nuisance and a hazard. Their children are against it. But for once, Maury and I agree. We both wish the woman were Ma.

April 26

She refuses to open her eyes, to speak. She's closed off from us and the world, drawn into herself either out of anger or exhaustion; she will not acknowledge Maury's efforts.

Why do I expect her to be responsive because I suddenly show up? If she doesn't acknowledge my presence this time, do I "punish" her by not coming again?

April 30

Aging. Pain in every joint. Loosening of flesh. Ringing in the ears. Slackening of skin. Rattling of teeth. Weakness of memory. No one can feel them except yourself. No one feels another's pain. How life breaks down when the body doesn't function perfectly. And at the center sits the child who never changes, who wonders how this could happen. Wake up, Claire, who are you talking about? Myself—I can't get out of bed this morning; is it the flu?

May 8

Two items from a local paper:

*l. A fifty-four-year-old Oregon woman with "a lust for life" ends
her own when she learns she has Alzheimer's. She's treated by a
doctor with a newly invented device in his van: three fluid-filled
bottles stop her heart quickly and painlessly. From his short bio
the unemployed doctor sounds like a compassionate man. He says
it is society that makes him into a Frankenstein.*

*2. The parents of Nancy Cruzan, comatose for seven years, want
to terminate her tube-feedings. The case is brought before the
Supreme Court who find "a lack of evidence" that Nancy willfully
agrees with her parents' decision. The feedings continue.*

And Claire, what would you do, cowardly wait out the bitter end? Is that
truly the best kind of courage to show "for the family's sake"?

May 10

We've got a new dog! Despite all our protestations, Amy convinced us to
adopt Sheba from the SPCA where she works. Lori, whose new role is
family therapist, says she sees a change in Maury's behavior when she
visits: "You know, Mom, all that love and attention Dad's trying to load on
Grandma isn't working; now he has Sheba. Dad's the type who needs
someone to need him."

Everyone agrees that Maury is more lively these days than he's been in a
long time.

May 13, Mother's Day

The only present we bring this year is Sheba. As soon as she enters the
Manor, her cheerful yipping and tail-wagging stop; she drops her head.
Can this be the same puppy who's so full of life and joy when Amy runs
with her? Sheba managed to spark a few smiles in two residents, but Ma
wouldn't even look at her.

May 15

Last night during yoga meditation, my teacher told us to envision some-one who needed healing and to see that person in white healing light, then to let go. I let go, Ma, only you're still there, you hang on.

May 21

Lori's final application to study in London next semester has come through! Can it be that a whole year of school has passed again? How will we ever be able to leave Ma this fall to visit her?

June 7

Drive right by, why go in? Arnold doesn't call, come to visit. When's the last time Ma heard from him? Never mind his personal problems—why should you care, she's not your mother. Forget it. She's erected a wall of silence around herself anyway. Maybe an angry one, a protective one, maybe one of dignity and pride, the only way she can cope with this terrible process. Whatever, don't go in. Go home for a walk instead on this beautiful spring day.

"Hello, Ma, it's Claire. I came to visit."

I touch her hair, pat her face, take her hand. "Would you like to sit outside?" No answer.

"Would you like something to eat?" No answer.

"It's so nice out. Can you see the pretty red plant on the balcony?" No answer.

"Amy misses you." No answer.

"I love you, Ma." No answer.

I leave, tears spot my new sundress I've worn to show I'm alive with the new season.

June 15

Today I'm going no matter what anyone else in this family does, even if she won't open her eyes, won't talk, even if she's slipping over to the other realm.

A sad visit. The only good thing about it is a glimpse of the retired doctor and the Berkeley professor sitting in a quiet corner holding hands.

June 20

A twenty-five-year-old woman in yoga class was killed in a freak accident. Our teacher quietly announces, "It was time for Jennifer to leave us. We never leave before we accomplish our purpose here on earth. Some people fulfill that goal earlier than others. Jennifer was like that. She lived more in twenty-five years than some people live in fifty. I feel a sense of completion for her with her death."

And I feel a sense of horror. Why do exceptional people seem to go first? And how could Ma's long decline have any possible "purpose" to it?

June 21, 1:00 A.M.

We never leave before our time, before we accomplish our purpose here on earth. These thoughts have haunted me all night. Earlier on the phone, when I told Fran about Jennifer's death, she swore, "God's a bitch."

July 8

Dream: Maury pulls his hair. "They won't feed her; they want her to die."

"If you weren't so attached to her, she'd let go. You weren't like this when we first married."

"She didn't need me then, don't you understand?"

I walk away. "You've become bent over, lifeless. I'm leaving."

"Go ahead."

I walk in the streets bent over. When I try to talk to people, they push me. "Get away, you're old. You don't know anything."

July 24

For three weeks, I've made a conscious decision not to visit. Finally, this morning I realized how stupid that was. The only one I'm hurting is myself. Told Maury I'd visit with him today if he liked.

"She's not responsive. Stay home."

Okay, I will. I've nothing more I can give her anyway.

August 27

Lori's getting ready for her trip. We don't talk about her coming back in case Grandma dies. She's filled with plans and excitement. I was surprised when she mentioned Ma at all.

"I'm part of this family, and I want to know what's going on," she demands.

I'm desperate to visit her in London this fall. When it's my time to die, I don't want to look back on my life thinking of all the things I never did. Yet another part of me begins to accept limitations: I may not be able to go.

September 3, Labor Day

All the kids home, except Lori. Like *Dinner at the Homesick Restaurant,* I can never get everyone under one roof. I need them around more than they need me. Jon brought Linda. In five minutes flat, I began to play Supermom wanting to please.

We all stopped in to see Ma and were sad when she didn't talk. Afterward, our own conversation centered on her silence.

Karen: "Maybe it's hard for her to form words. She always was guarded; she didn't even talk much when she first lived with us."

Jon: "With all those strokes she's been having, she can't talk. She doesn't recognize us."

Amy: "Then how come she smiled at me?"

Linda: "My grandma died after she stopped talking." (If she and Jon marry, how can we bring Ma to their wedding?)

And Maury. "But she *did* talk today. When a nurse tried to remove some scales, Grandma yelled, 'What do you think you're doing?' "

Our mouths dropped opened. The first sentence in months. Just as I suspected. She's been cognizant all along.

September 17

Today in yoga our teacher spoke of a "good death." At first I thought she meant a quick death, one without pain, but she explained, "The dying person doesn't fight death once she learns it's inevitable; neither does she blame others for not saving her. She accepts it as part of life."

126

I suppose there's a time when we stop raging and forget Dylan Thomas's "Do not go gentle into that good night."

Is that what Ma is trying to do with her silence?

September 21

Lori left for her semester in London today. I bawled my head off. The whole world lies before her. Ma seems like a remote "unnecessary object" next to her. Days pass with a speed that I've never known before. I'm going to visit my daughter whether Maury comes or not.

September 29

Jon and Linda announced their engagement tonight! We'll have to delay our trip to London. Everything's happening so fast. They're getting married the end of this year! Me, a mother-in-law, like Ma. Jon, a married man; Jonathan who was always so stubborn, his socks piled up in his room, rock blaring from his stereo. He's still so young. How will it be to connect with Linda's family, a whole group of people I don't know? Thank God they'll have a small wedding. It will solve problems with inviting all our relatives; they'll probably be furious when they don't receive invitations!

September 30

Got so involved with the kids on Yom Kippur I missed visiting Ma. To make up for it, this morning I rushed to the Manor with Maury. We were held up by roadwork. When we arrived, she was asleep. Maury phoned his siblings from the hall telephone. Arnold was "shocked" to hear Ma spends less than two hours a day out of bed, neither opens her eyes nor speaks. If he bothered to call, he'd know.

October 9

Amy insists we all try another visit with Sheba.

"You'll see, she'll be a friendlier dog with me there. I'll show her what to do." Amy and dog come along with us. Sheba refuses to go in. Finally we drag her up to Ma. She sniffs and weakly wags her tail, but Ma won't look at her.

On our way home, Amy's upset. "I was sure Sheba would cheer Grandma up. What's wrong? Is she comatose?"

Maury answers, "Of course not. She still responds, she eats and swallows; she squeezed your hand, didn't she?"

Silently "little" Amy, the only one of our four children left at home, walks out of the room.

October 10

My neighbor, Beverly Willis, and her brother have filed papers declaring their mother destitute and put her small savings in their names. Now the old woman has been placed in a state facility. No guilt, no bad feelings.

"Is it hard for you to visit her?" I ask.

"Why? At ninety-one, what else can I ask for? We were sucked dry of all our funds."

October 21

Maury has agreed to visit Lori in London! He phoned Helen and she's willing to come and stay here for a week. Feeling so grateful toward her. Our minds are eased enormously. He told me if Ma dies, we won't try to fly home for the funeral. Don't believe it; I think we should plan to, anyway. A cloud hangs over our heads; it's been there a long time, and who knows for how much longer? We can't keep delaying everything we want to do for fear she'll die while we're gone. I'd like to go right after Jon and Linda's wedding.

October 25

Reading about nineteenth-century England and how dying was a communal affair; it took place in public. Friends and passersby would crowd into the dying person's room to escort him and ease his way unto death.

October 26

> *You and I alone my love together we ferry across the Irish Sea /*
> *we with our unfulfilled ambitions / if only travel wouldn't evapo-*
> *rate into air / if only we could hold countries / in our pockets / live*
> *in two at a time / if only we could hold onto a souvenir / a poem in*
> *the tube / a daffodil a daughter or two / each other / ourselves*

November 8

Couldn't bear this visit even though the hallways have been renovated and were "cheerful." According to Maury she was "better" than last week.

Better. Her hair, the most unkempt I've seen it, was wild about her head, her eyes slightly opened. When I entered the room, she closed them and wouldn't look at us. Maury fed her from the syringe. This time I didn't touch her. How long her dying is.

November 16

Don't think we can really leave Ma and go to London at this time.

November 22, Thanksgiving

Maury visits Ma alone. I stay home to cook. No one asks about her; no one talks about her. But one of our guests bores us with stories on the care of her own mother, how much it has taken out of her, how consumed, how bitter she is. I never want to become like that.

At last I begin to speak about Ma, talk about her kindness, her strength. I become soft, teary eyed...then let my guest take me over with her bitterness. How bitterness begets bitterness. I get up from the table, busy myself in the kitchen, and don't say another word all night.

December 1

From William Styron's *Darkness Visible: A Memoir of Madness*: scholars are mystified by the suicide of Primo Levi, as this man whom they admired and who endured so much at the hands of the Nazis crumbled like he did. Some now say his death was accidental, but others rumored that at sixty-seven he had been heavily burdened by caring for his aged, paralytic mother, which was more spiritually oppressive than even his experience in Auschwitz. Preposterous—or not?

December 2

My parents arrive in ten days for Linda and Jon's wedding. Dad's got to get out of the cold, and staying at our house not only saves them money, we can keep an eye on them as well. We've had to cancel our plans for England. Incredibly disappointed at first, but now I've begun to accept it.

December 9

Dream: I'm sitting in an old Victorian house in San Francisco, holding a mirror to my face: wrinkles, brown spots, lines I've never seen before appear. I want desperately to get up from this "boudoir," but my knees are crippling me. Two

strangers enter the room "Oooh, I can't move," I moan. "Yes, you can. Just use
willpower." One shouts angrily, "Get up and walk!" The second follows suit,
"You're as good as dead." I remain speechless, holding the mirror.

They leave. I manage to climb onto my bed where I open a magazine and read,
"The average caretaker watches over her charge for twenty years." I flip the
pages. Terms zoom out at me: stocks, bonds, CDs, retirement, insurance, estate
taxes, home equity, nursing home insurance, everything I deplore thinking
about.

December 12

Mom and Dad arrived for a three-week stay, Mom with tears, Dad cheerful but with a bloody nose which apparently bled throughout the entire
flight. The minute he deplaned, we drove him straight to the emergency
room. Now he's got such a huge bandage on it, he looks comical. They
still think of me as "their little girl," while I see them in need of protection.

This morning Dad insisted on visiting Hilda. She's just fractured her arm
from what Maury calls "improper care," brittle bones, and plain fragility.
All this a week before the wedding.

Dad brought her a bright green pillow to make her room feel more
homey. I'm in my don't-let-anything-interfere-with-my-life mood; still,
liked Dad's thoughtfulness bringing something colorful.

Odd seeing Dad standing over my mother-in-law's bed and attempting
conversation with her: "Hi, Hildy, it's your old-time boyfriend, Jake.
Remember me?"

December 13

Mom and Dad have begun to decline. Dad still has good spirits, but how
rigid and dependent Mom's become. I worry how she'll get along without
him.

Rigidity doesn't have to be a natural condition of age, I keep telling myself. Remember reading about a Canadian artist and naturalist, Emily Carr, who wrote that she opened up and expanded as she grew older. Want to make sure the same happens to me.

December 14

Brought my dress for the wedding to a dressmaker's for alterations today. There sitting on a sofa quietly sat the dressmaker's mother, a tiny woman pulling at her lip. She's well into her nineties and very wrinkled, but still with perfect hearing.

Asked Mrs. Santiago how long her mom had been living with her.

"Oh, about eight years, but it's fine; you know, she doesn't bother anyone and is healthier than me. She just sits on the couch most of the day and watches me sew. When I go out, my sister stays with her. She'll outlive us all!"

Hmm. The very thing that was hard for me—having Ma sit around doing nothing and watching me!

December 15

Grandma and Grandpa are playing gin in the kitchen. God knows what they'll do without each other. In his ancient maroon sweater Grandpa, who's not looking so hot, takes a schnapps in the pantry. He has chest pains again. Neither of them go outside to see the California sunset; walking's too hard, but they're alert, content. They've lived to see their first grandson marry. Family is the whole of their lives.

When they finish, Grandma wanders into Karen's old room where she picks up *Pissing in the Snow and Other Ozark Folktales*, carries it back into the kitchen with a red face. "What's this world coming to?" Before we can answer, she rushes over to answer the phone everyone's ignoring.

"Helloo, helloo, I'm sorry I can't stop this crazy machine. I hate these answering things." She ends up recording her own voice. Later, I remove the tape to save it, without her knowing. How alike the women in our family sound.

Jon and Linda arrive; Grandpa brightens and teases him. "You young buck, c'mere and gimme a kiss. Take some schnapps. In a few days you'll need it more than me!" Of course the young couple can't stay, and within fifteen minutes they're gone. Grandpa's back at the TV nursing another violent death, all the time waiting for his own. Grandma starts scrubbing one of my pots that will never be as clean as hers. She reminisces about her wedding and my own.

"Claire, don't you hear me?"

"Hmm, oh yes, Mom, yes," I lie, too caught up in a hundred emotions to respond.

December 19

Under this canopy I'm numb, deaf, and dumb. Is this man Jon, the same Jon who sold his TV set for a keg of beer, the same kid who played hooky? I never laughed at your tricks like your grandmas. How you overwhelmed me, my firstborn. I didn't know what to expect. Oooh, my nose running. Any moment I'll become a character out of *Fiddler on the Roof*, anarchist mother in her ivory dress. No one sees the anarchy; I've hidden it under purple eyeliner. My face cracking from the strain, nose quivering on this full note of ancient Hebrew melody when love and marriage are so elevated that God and Israel are one. Then there was purity, which will die the minute this ceremony ends. Linda's parents, I barely know them. Are we putting on a good show for one another? I lean into Maury. Steady Maury, always around, always in that same conservative suit. Grandma and Grandpa Hirsch so proud, Grandpa worrying, "What will they live on?" Grandma Pearl is upset that more relatives from our side didn't come. It's all right, Mother, and it's okay that there aren't more flowers. Flowers cost so much more now than they did when I was married. Poor Grandma Hilda; although she lived, her body couldn't make it. Wanted the kids to stop at the Manor dressed in their wedding clothes, but Linda said it felt "unlucky."

1991

Hilda bustles in with bright, brown eyes

January 3, 1991

My parents left today. Even though Mom helped, all the cooking was driving me crazy. How did women of the last generation do it? Always wonder: Is this our last visit? Recently read we spend our childhood wanting to please our parents, our adolescence rebelling from them, and our adulthood trying to make peace with them. Don't die, Mamma; don't die, Daddy. Who will sit at my table, who will tell me bad from good, who will hold this baby life in their hands?

Midnight

How will I mourn you when you die? Let it be quickly, mercifully, an airplane crash. What is it, Dad? If I come to you and kiss you we'll both break into tears, hurt Mom, make her feel outside our love.

Anne Sexton: "A woman *is* her mother. That's the main thing."

Damn it, don't make me break down. Mom, Dad, I'm both of you—both.

January 4

Today was my first class in the Learning Center for one short term that ends in March; lots of cutbacks. Then I won't have any work the rest of the semester. How many times have I tried to "invent courses," spent hours dreaming up ideas, preparing, only to find I didn't get enough enrollment and have them canceled. But I can't give up; I must keep trying.

January 9

A hundred bucks for two. The salesgirl, a kid from my class who knows more about jackets than I do, talked me into it: "You won't find Liz Claiborne for that price." I didn't want them. Still, maybe jackets will say my days are filled with decisions even if they aren't, that I fly to meetings and give papers even if I don't. Two of them because I couldn't make up my mind. Conservative, masculine. One solid, one plaid. Two I lugged home, hung in the closet, all the time knowing I'd never wear them.

January 10

I do not think of her; I do not visit; her silence is too much to bear.

January 12

Ran into Beverly Willis. Her mother died quickly, didn't last long in the nursing home. How calm Bev was telling me that the two of them never got along that well; she certainly doesn't flagellate herself. "It's better off this way," is all she said.

January 14

Maury's thrown himself into work around the house. Redoing this place is an escape for him not to think of Ma so much. Hoped one day we'd move to the city, but he's determined to stay here. He's beginning to worry whether we'll have enough room for grandchildren!

Where else can we go? And after all these years, how will we ever clean out the garage?

January 15

Karen home for a break. She plans on going straight through graduate school and on for a Ph.D. Regretfully, I'm reminded of my own failed plans. Daughters today not only have the opportunities, they have the drive.

"Some women aren't made to be nursemaids, Mom. You're modern, not old-fashioned like Dad," she tries to soothe my doubts, but I wonder if it's not meant as a double entendre: *she's* the modern woman who won't have time for me.

Such changes in my offspring. Do they have any of their old childish attachment to Grandma Hilda left?

Go, my girl, do for your mom what she couldn't do for herself.

January 16

We're at war in the Gulf—I can't believe it.

January 20

Why didn't I go to the protest on the war? Am I putting my head in the sand, a coward who doesn't know what she believes? Is this what most Americans do, then wonder why we have so many problems as a nation?

January 28

Today my students brought in four editorials on Nancy Cruzan, who died after being kept alive in a vegetative state for eight years.

Controversy raged, such strong feelings about who should make ethical decisions. They lost their usual apathy. We discussed the Patient Self-Determination Act. Now hospitals and nursing homes that get medicaid or medicare would have to inform patients about the right-to-die options. Terry Miller, who's usually bored, wants the address of *The Harvard Medical School Health Letter;* it furnishes information for living wills and health proxies.

As the twenty-first century creeps up, my own kids will have control over their deaths.

February 4

A tasteless radio commercial for a new "posh" nursing home. One air-head-sounding socialite talking to another, "Oh dear, I don't know what to do with Mum."

"Why not put Mum into the Fountain of Youth Retirement Community? They have a plush beauty salon on the grounds, and she'll even have her own entertainment right there. She'll age gracefully at the Fountain."

I snap the radio off. "Aging gracefully"—what does *that* mean? Don't make waves, don't worry about the world too much, give up trying to accomplish what's hard for you? Above all, look youthful?

Lately I get angry when my mother bemoans her "fate" and gloomily admits she can't do what she used to do five years ago.

Hmm. Easier for me to be feisty with Mom than it ever was with Ma.

February 8

The students in this short-term class are older and highly motivated. When I finish it, guess I'll have a lot of time to explore some new avenues. Too much time.

February 11

The war continues...

February 12

Five weeks since my last visit. What's happening to me? Something inside yells, "Why won't you go?" But there's no voice that answers.

February 13

> *I grow old / I grow old / Shall I color my hair gold / like my mother / Wear a strap upon my chin / Leave my husband / Take a lover / Rub my knuckles thin*

2:00 A.M.

> *between dream and sleep / he slips into your netherworld / and brings it up to light / with eyes and arms / he stirs you / soothes you / do not touch him / except to grasp his hand / and fall backward / into times of troubadours / and courtly love / lithe dancer / dressed in High Renaissance / in this world / words glide / up from the sea / planetary music / hums about your head / in the morning he is gone*

Even Ma's illness hasn't totally snuffed out my own romantic fantasies—a place to escape when under family stress. I'll probably end up like one of those old, childlike females in the Manor crying about my lost youth and lost loves of sixty years ago.

February 15

Behaving like an adolescent, wanting nothing but my personal freedom, moody, escaping into fantasy. At noon walked Sheba into the last undeveloped section of this suburb. Healing for me, helped me to gain perspective. A war's on, Claire, something greater than you and your family. This isn't a time to accomplish anything.

Yet I must in order to live what I consider a fulfilling life.

February 18

I visited today. No response. I left after fifteen minutes.

February 20

From an old issue of *Time* magazine: an elderly man was driven across the border into Idaho where he was dumped at a dog-racing track—there are no laws against abandoning old people in that state.

February 27

Ran into Anna in town today. We were surprised to see each other. She now has a little girl and is expecting again. She was sad to hear that Hilda ended up in a nursing home.

"I thought she could make it on her own with some help," she sighed.

She began talking about Ma. Finally we went into La Petite Boulangerie and finished chatting over muffins and tea.

"Remember that time I got stuck with her over a weekend? I didn't want to say no, but I was lonely and needed to cheer up. So I went out and bought a ham and cooked a fancy dinner. Only I tell Hilda it's turkey. All the time I say how great is this turkey, she says nothing. When she finishes, she smacks her lips, 'Anna, that's the best kosher ham I ever ate.'"

We both laughed with tears in our eyes.

"A good woman, Hilda. My first lady when I come from the Philippines, the best lady I ever work with. Funny, smart. I liked her—only I couldn't stay overnight. That was too hard for me."

March 1

Tonight I listened to three street poets read on lust, poverty, cowardliness, bravery, and the Gulf War. So many people dying. Even the animals in the Iraqi zoo are eating each other as the war continues and no one nurtures them. Can't bear reading the paper.

March 13

Picked up Norman Cousins's *Anatomy of an Illness*. Although I read it years ago, it's more meaningful now. He's onto the American overuse of medicine and the interaction of mind and body. Loved his chapters "Creativity and Longevity" and "Pain Is Not the Ultimate Enemy." He quotes those octogenarians whose drive and ability to laugh at themselves keeps them alive for years. And his chapter on learning to live with pain is a classic.

March 15

Found some of my old notes on Camus's diaries dated 1970. Browsed through them and came across: "A fear of life is a fear of death." I remember how struck I was with that entry, and more than twenty years later, still am.

March 16

My class has ended. Not to be lost in work…maybe it's okay. Come on, Claire, who are you kidding…you're just like Mom!

March 20

How silent the house; Maury and Amy both away. I'm here alone, except for Sheba. If Ma had come now instead of four years ago, could I have handled the situation differently? Then it was everything at once; now the quiet is eerie and the house, cavernous.

Then I needed a few days alone during the week, short breaks for myself. I guess from now on I'll have many days like this.

March 23

I've begun to study t'ai chi to learn to center myself better. Not sure how it works, but it does because I feel a calmness in my body. If I go to class, I'm better able to cope.

There's so much out there—easy to get distracted. Best to stick with one thing, make a commitment to it, not jump frantically from option to option.

April 6

Am enjoying t'ai chi immensely. Through it, I've become interested in Zen. Lately I devour every book about the subject that I can get my hands on. Can't stop reading. Feeling more positive, capable of moving in my life, more content despite existing difficulties.

April 7

A new idea for teaching struck me last night. Maybe it came to me because I've stopped trying so hard and allowed myself to relax. I'm going to put a course proposal together for the fall.

April 9

Reading, reading, reading. Ernest Becker's *The Denial of Death,* Scoop Nisker's *Crazy Wisdom;* two very different books, but both are making an impact on me. If there's a time for each season, this must be the time for in-gathering.

Later, maybe I'll go out more, but for now, I stay home, sit in the yard and read; then I walk to digest what I've read, and see if California poppies await me on the hillsides.

April 13

When did it seem the kids would never grow up? Now I wonder how I did everything with all of them here. Today I'm restless, wish Amy were around.

Last night Maury and I sat across the kitchen table from each other, alone, barely conversing. What will our lives be like after Amy leaves? And that won't be too long. Now we'd have plenty of room for Ma.

April 20

"I don't have a profession," I tell Maury, still not adjusted to my free time.

"You have a discipline; you've a couple of them—writing in your diary and t'ai chi classes."

Okay, I have a discipline, a couple of them. Here's a hug, baby. That's the best thing you've said to me in years—and I love you for it.

April 26

I have allowed Claire Brenner to spend a whole day at a beautiful and peaceful place, Green Gulch Farm-Zen Center fifteen minutes from Muir Beach. Brenner sat silently in the zendo and felt calmness seep into her body to strengthen her. Told her she can change her reality, handle crises in a more detached way; difficult for someone who's only beginning to live in the moment, to appreciate the late winter rains, to get turned down from a job and know it's not the end of the world.

April 28

This morning we become lovers; don't rush, we've plenty of time, we without glasses, masks, our toes interlocking, this new little belly. How you've pushed me to confront my weaknesses. How I nearly let myself become nothing. You never understood why I couldn't have Ma. You've never known how hard it is for me to hold onto all my parts. How she became a force between us. I wanted to run from you, but wherever I ran, I found that part of you that's me. Now I give myself over to you. The thought terrifies. Must not need you too much. The sun rises. The phone rings. Look, our wedding picture above our bed, me with my tiny pearl crown, squinting out of my contact lenses, you, even then, with that look of responsibility on your beneficent forehead.

April 29

Visited for ten minutes today. There's nothing I can do about Ma's situation. I've stopped agonizing—maybe t'ai chi and my readings have helped.

May 1

Four back issues of *The New York Times* pile up on the table: imagine, to a whole generation growing up, Martha Graham won't seem real, as if she never lived. She'll become a vague name. Once something dies, does it become a shadow of itself? Can it no longer truly exist?

And buried in the middle of the paper, an article on a Viennese nurse of "mercy" who killed forty-two people in a Vienna convalescent home and is now being charged with murder.

The daily events of the world lie around the house and end up in news-print to be recycled into a never-ending cycle of more newsprint.

May 5

I behold the golden hillsides, such incredible beauty.

May 9

All my friends are so busy with careers and earning money. What about me?

Gaining inner peace is what counts now. How to get it, how to hold onto it. My writing seems more important than ever.

May 16

> *This morning / when I bathed / my body / I found her / a rare gift / in the early half-light / dappled old pony / under the shower / She was near perfect / two pounds lighter / than last week / from: dancing / yes / dancing! / when I made her / pick up her monster feet / and tear them / loose / Now I looked her over / and saw an age spot on her brow / I kissed it / dressed her in freewheeling clothes / and walked her / out into the gorgeous day / while the Soviets are crumbling / the rain forest dying / Grandma might die / and this mood will not last / Her happiness made me say / Hello / to everyone / old people / dogs / Her happiness filled me with love/ and made me / not care what anyone / thought / of her / or me / It made us both so happy / we nearly cried*

May 18

Cleaned the house all weekend—Karen is coming home with her new boyfriend, Ron. Started fussing in the kitchen, then cleaned out the bathroom cabinets, and what did I find? The extra pair of dentures that belongs to Ma, the ones she hated. I never even knew she had them here. She still permeates the air in our house.

May 20

Karen's here with Ron. She's so young and lovely, he's so handsome; the delicate loss of self and the endless scramble to regain it. Karen who has no time to kiss me. I ask her if she wants to help me pick out a new sofa bed after Ron leaves.

"What's this sudden interest in material stuff? You never cared before."

"I know, but everything's getting so shabby. That couch is twenty years old. If I replace my furniture, someday you'll be able to use it."

"Mom, you don't need to achieve immortality through possessions. I'll buy my own couches with my own taste. Maybe you better go back to work to keep your mind occupied."

So you see through my ploy. Your mother is cunning in her ways of wanting to be remembered.

May 22

> *When the old master / folded my fingers / inside his / when he squared my hips / and pierced my eyes / when he in the old grey coat and cotton shoes / molded the air / my mind split from my body / and I was not one with the moment / in his touch was something / I wanted to give back to him / I cursed my youth and*

age / I cursed my mind for stopping / short of real learning / but
bowed to the master / who went home to Chinatown / while I went
home to the suburbs / with the sweet pain of Tuesday nights

May 23

Ma is very ill; Maury has a "plan" to bring her back to Saint Louis and stay with her at Helen's until she dies. I say nothing. Nor do I blame Helen for what I know her decision will be. Of course he is unrealistic. Maybe somewhere he could do it. It is possible to bring a dying person home, isn't it?

May 24

Dream: Maury boards a plane with Ma. The passengers think she's a mummy and get off. All the pilots disembark; he's alone. He's got to man the engine himself. He's gone for days flying and flying and getting nowhere because Ma is growing stronger and more invincible every minute.

May 28

Ten days until my fiftieth birthday, and this morning I received my first acceptance since my twenties—my story about Ma will be published in *Moment!* After initial jubilation, I felt shaky. What will it mean to get something I've wished for so long?

Calm yourself, Claire. Five minutes in the sun blinds you into thinking you'll become rich and famous. Just keep working and don't worry about the end results. The world won't love you anymore; maybe you'll make a few friends, but bet you'll lose more over going public. Your whole life isn't going to change. The story doesn't matter to anyone but you, and if you keep thinking it does, you're a fool.

May 29

Yeah, but life is short, art is long.

May 31

Still feeling high from my acceptance, such validation, and in a way, for such a small thing. But isn't it true that I'm least fragmented, most able to pull all the pieces of my life together when alone at the computer, especially when the work goes well? Makes all the difficulties, all the frustrations worthwhile.

June 1, 7:00 A.M.

> *converging of diary and dreams / merging of palm and fingertip / a world to fathom / bright and dark / oh the fear and joy of receiving / your secret message / stealing me from the kingdom of other / charming my heart / with what I've known all along / to drag you up to surface / and spread you among my being / a rare drink / a fine fruit / you have been long in coming / with many detours on the way / years ago I sat in a park / flirting with your face in a pond / not knowing how to reach you / your slow rhythm / has waited to release its form / do not leave me / to fall back into emptiness / to live off my top layer / close one eye / so both go weak / and my vision splinters / stay fullness / prism of light / stay and show me the whole*

June 5

Seems like I'll never write another thing. Amazing how we can't hang on to anything.

June 6

She's a bit better. Maury's given up his Saint Louis plan.

Went to visit. She won't talk, but for some reason, I didn't mind today. Held her hand for a while. Did I imagine a slight smile on her lips?

June 7

Miss my students reminding me of what it's like to be young. We've become so ghettoized according to age. Even miss those two punk rockers who stared at me across the aisle of their youth as if I were some potential ancient enemy.

June 8, 5:00 A.M., My Birthday

> *Let my cake sweeten / the repose of my life / let its candles / light up my soul / knowing I've lived / the only way I could / let me prepare these words / a table set before me / in my own presence / to comfort myself / when my cup runs empty / let me offer them up*

June 9

Went with Maury; my last few months of stubbornness have passed. No matter how hard he tries, talks about the kids, their schooling, their adventures, she won't open her eyes, smile, respond, take his hand. I stroked her cheek and her hair this time. As long as the aides get a bit of water and food into her, she continues to hang on. He simply can't bring himself to tell them to stop.

"There's a difference between denying and not offering if she asks," he says.

June 10

Maury's been accepted for a stress-control program for men at the Meyer Friedman Institute! *I'm* the one who pushed him into this. The study discusses how emotions related to time urgency and hostility cause stress and disease. In some ways, Maury's not Type A (and I am!), but he is compulsive about work.

Don't die, kid, and leave me a widow. I already have three friends who are widows; noticed that all of them use coping mechanisms they learned *before* they were widowed, not after.

June 11

A cyclone in Bangladesh killed 139,000, thousands of homeless among the Kurdish refugees in Iraq, and Ma—down to eighty-nine pounds. Won't eat when she's well enough to remember not to. Too numb to feel anything, even anger at "God's mysterious ways."

June 12

According to Sizzler's, I'm now a senior citizen and qualify for a discount at their salad bar! Yuck!

June 13

Think I'll run away—and haunt the shopping mall.

June 14

Menopause creeping up right on schedule. Seems as if I were just forty. But fifty! And still many unresolved issues. How is it that I thought I'd never get as old as my parents?

Can't imagine what I'll look like at sixty. No face-lift or liposuction. And after reading Sadja Greenwood's book, *Menopause, Naturally,* no estrogen either. I don't want to be "backward," but I just am not the type, and resent all the M.D.'s pushing it on me.

June 15

"Whaat! Your hair was just beginning to look decent. Why'd you cut it all off?"

No answer; I keep bugging him. Finally: "Because Ma will die within the month, and I wanted to cut it before then."

"Oh."

I'd forgotten the male injunction against hair cutting during the period of *shiva.*

He goes to the phone, calls Arnold, and tells him "to be prepared." Busy myself at the sink, hear him raise his voice.

"I won't do that. If you want a feeding tube put down her throat, you'll have to come here and do it yourself."

My craziness returns. I swear so loud Arnold can hear me. "The damn fool. Did he visit once? Did he? He has the gall to insist that the nurses do that!"

Maury holds his hand over the receiver. "I'll handle him. It's not your problem."

Damn him, damn Arnold, damn everything!

Just when I thought I was learning detachment.

June 16

So you want to sit around feeling sorry for yourself? You want to sit around and *nosh* Ak Mak and peanut butter all night and fast all the next while talking about food with friends? Not exactly "empty nest" syndrome. Amy's still here—for a few more weeks after high school graduation; then she takes off.

Don't put down "volunteering." You don't have to be a "socialite," and you aren't working. See how the novelty of publishing has worn off. Before this, whenever you had spare time, you always thought you needed to "save" Ma, but now...

Admit it; you've got to find more avenues that bring satisfaction.

June 20

Yesterday morning was the first time I'd ever worked at a church; I cut two hundred slices of bread, buttered and baked them, set out dessert, and served the unemployed—homeless or not. Tuesday, I'm tutoring a couple who recently arrived from Moscow. How different their lives from mine, their ways of coping.

June 23

In town today I met Lila.

"Claire, it's more than three years. You look different; you seem so much more at peace than when your mother-in-law first arrived."

Is it true? Is it because I've given up visiting?

June 24

Thought of having Linda's parents over for the Fourth, but too much of a "should." The same old question arises: how can you be honest to yourself without hurting others—and eventually yourself?

July 1

Dream: Ma's in the backyard with Jon. She calls me. I actually hear her voice. When I wake, I'm surprised she's not here.

July 2

A woman from the German department has invited me to a last minute women's celebration on the Fourth. Was surprised, as I haven't seen her in months. Hadn't made any plans, so I can go. Ursula, who's made a few small documentaries, asked me to bring along a reading. Glad it wasn't a cake I had to bake!

July 5

What an energizing day yesterday. All kinds of women talked about life in the nineties. Many changes, yet the basic theme remains—"wanting it all," independence *and* security.

Enacting an old goddess ritual, I touched a woman I'd never seen before on the space between her eyes. How much we were both prisoners of our bodies, unable to get beyond our flesh.

Toward evening, met a Canadian woman who talked about Canada's health system; Canadians must wait forever or travel far distances for specialists, but at least their medical care doesn't depend on their income.

July 7

> *today I have room / for all selves / they nestle / without jostling /*
> *those who love me / or each other / today black flowers grow wild /*
> *in my garden*

July 10

Good-bye Amy, you can hardly wait to leave. Too busy to visit Grandma? Okay, I understand. But what's happened to the high, sweet, rich voice you used to sing with when you jumped off the school bus, your socks slipping down into your shoes, your ragged ponytails flying in the wind? Where were they at your high school graduation last month? You'll be back late in August from your summer job, then it's off to college while I remain here in the house. No Jon, no Karen, no Lori, and now, no Amy. No Grandma Hilda. Will I go to the pool every day? Become a lawyer, a doctor, a housewife in tennis whites, a California jock?

July 16

Dream: I return home from a funeral, Maury's with me; we stay in a hotel whose rooms are decorated in corporate America design. The shiva is raucous with laughter and food; people don't stop eating and talking, I'm polite to everyone, including the rabbi's wife who wears a sheitel to cover her own hair. Suddenly, I leave and hurry back to the airport without Maury. The moving stairs play futuristic music, a medley of "Rhapsody in Blue" in a synthesized voice that repeats, "Keep moving; please keep moving." Instead of paying attention to the stairs, my eyes follow squares of graduated colors: red, blue, green, purple, and yellow with thin beams of colored light.

Helen appears; she reaches out, we hug. Mary Alice is behind her, demands Ma's pearls and samovar. Then I'm flying back home. As soon as I arrive, I phone Mary Alice and tell her we've used all Ma's money on the nursing home. She doesn't believe me. I receive a call from Maury. I'm to take the next plane back at once.

July 19

My darling Dad isn't feeling well; always feared all three of our parents getting sick at the same time. Dad's always snapped back before this. I hope to God he gets better soon.

July 24

Linda's pregnant! *Grandma.* I can barely write the word; I'm scared of it. What do grandmothers of my generation do? Wear gold charm bracelets with dangling charms named for their grandchildren like my mother did? Baby-sit their grandkids while their daughters-in-law go to work? Play Legos with them? Take them to the park? Certainly I'll be a different grandmother than Ma and my own mother. To think my folks will become great-grandparents.

July 25

The-farmer-in-the-dell, the-farmer-in-the-dell, tisket-a-tasket. Hello bobbing head with Jon's dark hair. Hello stories I read under cover with a flashlight; they're all coming back to me. Hello my own child self; I gratefully share it with you more than I could with my own children. What do grandmas do at fifty? They give their grandbabies what they couldn't give their own babies at twenty-three.

August 2

Long days—not much to do. Reread an essay by Malcolm Cowley, "Vices and Pleasures: The View from 80." Every word filled with wisdom, especially the closing paragraphs on how great thinkers outwitted infirmity: Renoir, by painting with a brush strapped to his arm when he was crippled by arthritis; Goya, by wearing spectacles on top of spectacles and using a magnifying glass; and Paul Claudel, who wrote in his journal, "No eyes left, no ears, no teeth, no legs, no wind! And when all is said and done, how astonishingly well one does without them!"

Astounding. I won't forget that one! It's already become part of me.

August 3

Our American naïveté, our lack of acceptance of age and death. Is fifty old? Sometimes when I look in the mirror, it seems I was never young, all those years vanished in thin air. Yet today I feel like a teenager.

August 4

Since Ma is hanging on much longer than we thought, dare we plan a week's vacation? We haven't been away the whole summer, but we're talking about a short weekend before Labor Day.

August 5, 1991

Up late browsing the news—Ted Kennedy pushes a shrunken Rose, 101, in a wheelchair; a fourteen-year-old boy afflicted with AIDS marries his sixteen-year-old girlfriend, saying how fast you grow up with this disease.

Then the kitchen phone rings at 11:50 P.M. I grab it.

Hilda Schneidman Brenner, mother of three, grandmother of ten, great-grandmother of nine, last surviving relative of the Schneidman and Brenner clan, died at 11:33 P.M. Must wake Maury. Should I wait until daylight? He needs his rest. I hesitate, walk slowly into our bedroom, wait a few minutes, touch him.

He rolls over. "Hmm."

"It's Ma."

He stirs, says nothing. Then at last, after a long garbled sigh and a catch in his throat: "I wasn't with her. They didn't call me, those damn fools. I didn't get a chance to shut her eyes."

I try to calm him. "Maybe a new nurse was on duty; maybe it happened too fast."

We sit together for a few minutes. I hold him. He wipes his face, goes to the phone, and starts making arrangements.

Our days are as grass; we flourish as a flower in the field; the wind passes over it, and it is gone.

August 6, 5:00 A.M.

> *You're suspended in air; beneath, no earth exists. The night is moist; space caves in. All her pain and suffering are over. All the love and anger dissolve—the way you remember a woman, that's her afterlife.*
>
> *You're young again, sitting around a big table in the old flat with your husband's relatives. They hug, kiss, and cry. Do business as usual. Deal and wheel. Everyone will die. You, your husband, your children, your unborn grandchildren. Now that you've come closer to death, you fear it less. Oh look! Hilda! She bustles in with bright, brown eyes, finely shaped nose, and keen mind. She takes her teeth out of her pocket and puts them in her mouth. She tells you she's cooking blintzes for everyone. What about the coroner, you hear Maury say with another part of you. No need for autopsy. It's a blessing. You have to tell the children. You have to find something to wear to the funeral. She's walking toward you. She smells of Christmas trees. You hear her voice, "Here, take a blintz, Claire darling, I filled them with the best cheese just for you. Take, they're good."*

159

About the Author

Elaine Marcus Starkman teaches English at Diablo Valley College and has also taught short-story writing for the University of California, Berkeley Extension. Her work keeps evolving with her life and her age. She has written both prose and poetry, including three plays and the lyrics for a musical narrative performed at Oberlin College. Elaine has been a student of t'ai chi for four years. She finds writing the one activity that totally engages her.

In 1990, she co-edited *Without a Single Answer: Poems on Contemporary Israel* (Judah Magnes Press). Her work has appeared in *Between Ourselves: Letters Between Mothers & Daughters* (Houghton Mifflin, 1983), *Vital Lines, St. Martin's Press, Kalliope, Filtered Images, Paper Only, Shaking Eve's Tree, JPS,* and *New Realities. The Best Time* (Sheer Press, 1992) is Elaine's fourth collection of poems.

Quality Books from Papier-Mache Press

At Papier-Mache Press our goal is to produce attractive, accessible books that deal with contemporary personal, social, and political issues. Our titles have found an enthusiastic audience in general interest, women's, new age, and Christian bookstores, as well as in gift stores, mail order catalogs, and libraries. Many have also been used by teachers for women's studies, creative writing, and gerontology classes, and by therapists and family counselors to help clients explore personal issues such as aging and relationships.

If you are interested in finding out more about our other titles, ask your local bookstores which Papier-Mache items they carry. Or, if you would like to receive a complete catalog of books, posters, and shirts from Papier-Mache Press, please send a self-addressed stamped envelope to:

Papier-Mache Press
135 Aviation Way, #14
Watsonville, CA 95076